Graphic Organizer Activities
with Answer Key

HOLT
THE AMERICAN NATION

HOLT, RINEHART AND WINSTON
A Harcourt Education Company
Austin • New York • Orlando • Atlanta • San Francisco • Boston • Dallas • Toronto • London

Cover: Peter Harholdt / Superstock
Title Page: © CORBIS/Bill Ross

Printed in the United States of America

ISBN 0-03-065331-2

3 4 5 6 7 8 9 082 04

Graphic Organizer Activities

To the Teacher

Each chapter of *The American Nation* has a graphic organizer activity that focuses on one aspect of chapter content. The graphic organizer activities provide you with a way to help students organize information. The different organizers allow you to meet the varied learning styles of students, and provide students with an alternative study aid. While activities in this handbook are designed for specific chapter content in *The American Nation,* you may use and adapt these graphic organizers as needed to fit other program content.

Name ______________________ Class ____________ Date ____________

CHAPTER 1

The World by 1500

GRAPHIC ORGANIZER ACTIVITY

Expanding Cultures Through Trade

Complete the time line. Describe an event or invention for each date indicated, and explain how it influenced trade and culture.

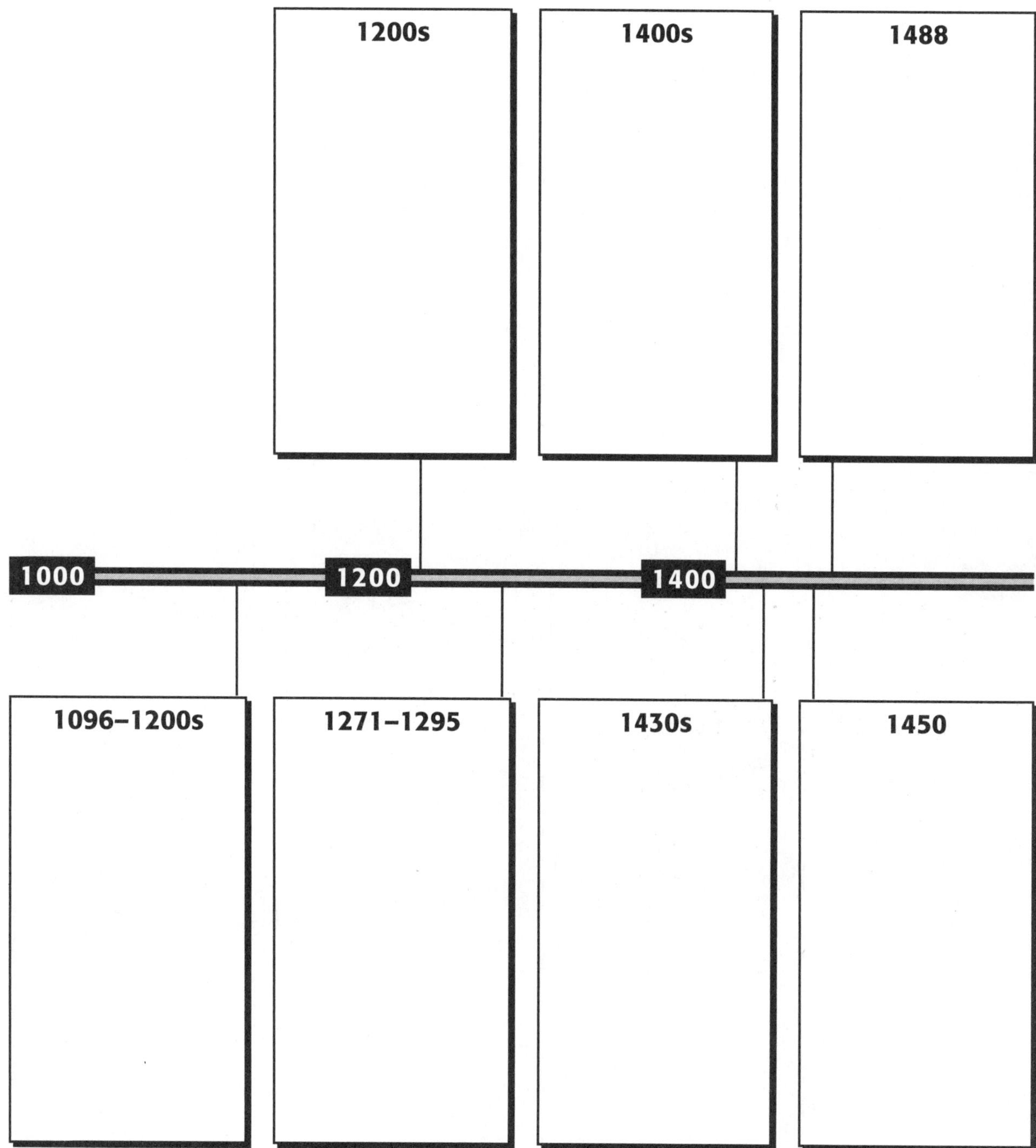

The World by 1500

GRAPHIC ORGANIZER: POSSIBLE SOLUTION

Expanding Cultures Through Trade

Complete the time line. Describe an event or invention for each date indicated, and explain how it influenced trade and culture.

1000 — 1200 — 1400

1096–1200s
The Crusades
- *introduces goods from Asia and the Middle East to Europe*

1200s
the compass
- *allows sailors to determine direction in all weather*

1271–1295
Marco Polo
- *travels to China, spends time in Chinese courts, and brings back tales of Asian splendor*
- *lures others to travel and trade*

1400s
Portuguese Caravels
- *more maneuverable ships, which increase sea trade*

1430s
Portuguese explorers along the African coast
- *trade for gold and expand culture*

1450
Gutenberg's press
- *movable type and books*
- *expand knowledge between cultures*

1488
Bartolomeu Dias rounds Cape of Good Hope
- *establishes sea route to Indian Ocean*
- *expands trade in India, Africa, and southern China*
- *spurs on other explorers and traders*

Name ______________________ Class ____________ Date ____________

Empires of the Americas

GRAPHIC ORGANIZER ACTIVITY

Spanish and English Exploration

Complete the graphic organizer by listing the dates and the exploration or conquest for which they are known.

	Explorers and Conquistadores	Date	Exploration or Conquest
SPAIN	Columbus		
	Balboa		
	Magellan		
	Cortés		
	Pizarro		
	de Soto		
	Coronado		
	Cabrillo		
	de Oñate		
	Serra		
ENGLAND	Cabot		
	Raleigh		
	Drake		

Empires of the Americas

GRAPHIC ORGANIZER: POSSIBLE SOLUTION

Spanish and English Exploration

Complete the graphic organizer by listing the dates and the exploration or conquest for which they are known.

	Explorers and Conquistadores	Date	Exploration or Conquest
SPAIN	Columbus	*1492*	*landed in Bahamas, Haiti, Dominican Republic*
SPAIN	Balboa	*1513*	*crossed the Isthmus of Panama*
SPAIN	Magellan	*1519*	*sailed around the tip of South America; his ships circumnavigated the world*
SPAIN	Cortés	*1519–22*	*explored Mexico; destroyed the Aztec civilization*
SPAIN	Pizarro	*1531–32*	*explored Central America; conquered the Inca*
SPAIN	de Soto	*1540s*	*explored the Mississippi*
SPAIN	Coronado	*1540s*	*marched through the Southwest*
SPAIN	Cabrillo	*1542*	*explored California coast*
SPAIN	de Oñate	*1598*	*first Spanish settlement in New Mexico*
SPAIN	Serra	*1700s*	*established missions in California*
ENGLAND	Cabot	*1497*	*landed in Newfoundland*
ENGLAND	Raleigh	*1585*	*sent colonists to Virginia*
ENGLAND	Drake	*1577*	*pirate; attacked Spanish ships in Americas; sailed to California coast*

Name ______________________ Class __________ Date __________

The English Colonies

GRAPHIC ORGANIZER ACTIVITY

Life in England's Colonies

Complete the graphic organizer by comparing life in the English colonies. Note similarities and differences between the northern and the southern groups, including topics such as family life, education, religion, economic status, conflicts, and commerce.

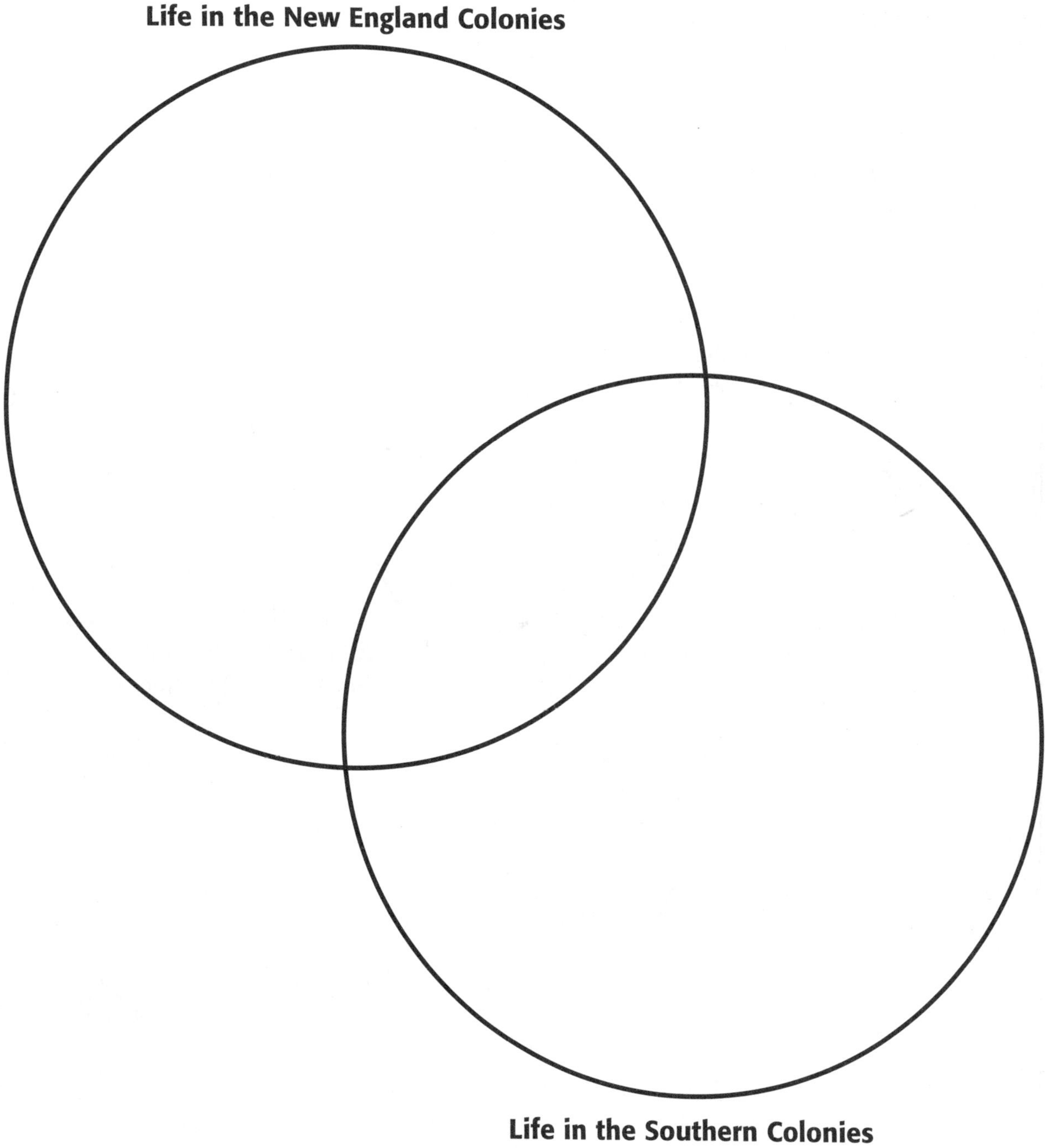

Life in the New England Colonies

Life in the Southern Colonies

The English Colonies

GRAPHIC ORGANIZER: POSSIBLE SOLUTION

Life in England's Colonies

Complete the graphic organizer by comparing life in the English colonies. Note similarities and differences between the northern and the southern groups, including topics such as family life, education, religion, economic status, conflicts, and commerce.

Life in the New England Colonies

- *children required to read to understand Bible*
- *large families, six to nine children or more*
- *men working as artisans or small farmers; some in fishing, trade, and business*
- *small farms that could be managed by large families*
- *religious tensions, witchcraft trials, belief in moral life*

- *arrived in colonies looking for better life*
- *sought religious freedom*
- *many farmers*

- *widespread rural areas with few towns or schools; education only for children of the wealthy, not of the poor*
- *conflicts between freed indentured servants, wealthy, and Indians for property*
- *immigrants mostly indentured servants, men and boys*
- *climate that bred disease, many deaths, small families*
- *slave class created by forbidding freedom, education*
- *large plantations that required many hands; gave rise to slavery*

Life in the Southern Colonies

Name ______________________ Class __________ Date __________

CHAPTER 4

Independence!

GRAPHIC ORGANIZER ACTIVITY

The Battle for Independence

Complete the chart by describing each British action and the colonists' response.

British action		Colonists' response
Sugar Act of 1764/Stamp Act of 1765 ______ ______	colonists respond by →	______ ______ ______
Townshend Acts ______ ______	colonists respond by →	______ ______ ______
Boston Massacre ______ ______	colonists respond by →	______ ______ ______
Massachusetts governors on payroll by decree of King George ______	colonists respond by →	______ ______ ______
Tea Act of 1773 ______ ______	colonists respond by →	______ ______ ______
Intolerable Acts of 1774 ______ ______	colonists respond by →	______ ______ ______
Quebec Act ______ ______	colonists respond by →	______ ______ ______
Attempt by General Gage to seize military supplies in Concord ______	colonists respond by →	______ ______ ______

Independence!

GRAPHIC ORGANIZER: POSSIBLE SOLUTION

The Battle for Independence

Complete the chart by describing each British action and the colonists' response.

British action		Colonists' response
Sugar Act of 1764/Stamp Act of 1765 *Britain begins enforcing import tax on foreign sugar, molasses, and other items.*	colonists respond by →	*Answers may include colonists feel left out of political process; assemble in protest; the Virginia House of Burgesses declares resolutions condemning the Stamp Act.*
Townshend Acts *Britain fixes duties on lead, tea, glass, dyes. Issues writs of assistance.*	colonists respond by →	*Colonists refuse to issue writs of assistance; women in Massachusetts make own cloth, refuse to drink tea; angry mob demonstrates.*
Boston Massacre *British soldiers open fire on crowd and kill five colonists.*	colonists respond by →	*Colonists write songs and poems for the dead; try soldiers for murder.*
Massachusetts governors on payroll by decree of King George *British attempt to gain control of colonial government.*	colonists respond by →	*Bostonians form 21-member Committee of Correspondence to inform colonists and the world.*
Tea Act of 1773 *British law excuses British East India Co. from paying certain duties and allows them to bypass wholesalers.*	colonists respond by →	*concern about monopoly; Sons of Liberty threaten anyone who would buy tea; colonists dump 342 chests of tea in the Boston Harbor.*
Intolerable Acts of 1774 *Answers may include British close part of Boston Harbor; revoke Massachusetts charter; forbid town meetings.*	colonists respond by →	*Other colonists send food and money to Massachusetts; colonists denounce George III's actions.*
Quebec Act *Britain extends its Canadian boundaries.*	colonists respond by →	*Colonists unite against British oppression; First Continental Congress; The Declaration of Resolves, which states power of legislature, ban on all trade with Britain.*
Attempt by General Gage to seize military supplies in Concord *A shot is fired. British troops kill colonists.*	colonists respond by →	*Patriots kill or wound 273 British soldiers, begin the Revolutionary War.*

Name ______________________ Class ____________ Date ____________

From Confederation to Federal Union

GRAPHIC ORGANIZER ACTIVITY

Checks and Balances

Complete the chart by listing powers delegated to the three branches of the United States government.

	Executive Branch	Judicial Branch	Legislative Branch
Who?			
Powers?	• • • • • • • • •	• • • • • • • • •	• • • • • • • • •

From Confederation to Federal Union

GRAPHIC ORGANIZER: POSSIBLE SOLUTION

Checks and Balances

Complete the chart by listing powers delegated to the three branches of the United States government.

	Executive Branch	Judicial Branch	Legislative Branch
Who?	*The President*	*The Supreme Court*	*The Congress*
Powers?	• *can veto bills passed by Congress* • *can curb congressional power through influence, pressure, and lobbying* • *can call Congress to deal with a national crisis* • *can pardon people convicted of federal crime* • *delivers annual State of the Union address* • *appoints judges and cabinet members*	• *can declare laws and executive actions unconstitutional* • *duty to interpret and uphold the Constitution* • *hold offices for life*	• *can check presidential power* • *2/3 vote of Senate needed to ratify treaties and constitutional amendments* • *advise and consent on appointments (Senate)* • *authorize moneys and approve federal budget* • *can propose constitutional amendments* • *can override president's veto with a 2/3 majority vote* • *approves federal judges (Senate)*

Name ______________________ Class __________ Date __________

CHAPTER 6

A Strong Start for the Nation

GRAPHIC ORGANIZER ACTIVITY

The Bill of Rights

Complete the graphic organizer by explaining in your own words each amendment in the Bill of Rights. Then explain the reason these rights were considered important in the late 1700s.

Bill of Rights

I

II

III

IV

V

VI

VII

VIII

IX

X

Reasons for the Bill of Rights

____

____

____

____

CHAPTER 6 A Strong Start for the Nation

GRAPHIC ORGANIZER: POSSIBLE SOLUTION

The Bill of Rights

Complete the graphic organizer by explaining in your own words each amendment in the Bill of Rights. Then explain the reason these rights were considered important in the late 1700s.

Bill of Rights

I *All people have the right to gather peacefully in religious or political groups. They also have freedom of religion, speech, press, and petition.*

II *States are allowed to keep troops; individual people to keep firearms.*

III *The government cannot order people to house soldiers except in times of war.*

IV *Police have to have a warrant, based on strong evidence, before they can search your property or person.*

V *No one can force you to testify against yourself; you must be read your rights when you are arrested; the government must pay for any property it takes.*

VI *Everyone will receive a fair trial. The government will provide a lawyer in criminal cases if you do not have one.*

VII *Everyone is entitled to a jury trial when the civil case is big enough to warrant it.*

VIII *You must be treated with fairness and decency even when accused of a crime.*

IX *Even if a right is not listed in the Constitution, people are still entitled to that right.*

X *States can pass laws on internal matters such as water rights, schools, roads, etc. as long as they are not unconstitutional or already governed by the federal government.*

Reasons for the Bill of Rights

Answers will vary; George III had attempted to rescind all individual rights in order to gain control of the colonies. Colonists were wary of a strong government and felt the new government should be constructed to support individual rights.

Name ______________________ Class ____________ Date ____________

Nationalism and Economic Growth

GRAPHIC ORGANIZER ACTIVITY

Jackson's Indian Policies

Write your opinion of Jackson's Indian policies. Before writing, use the graphic organizer to collect facts and examples from your text.

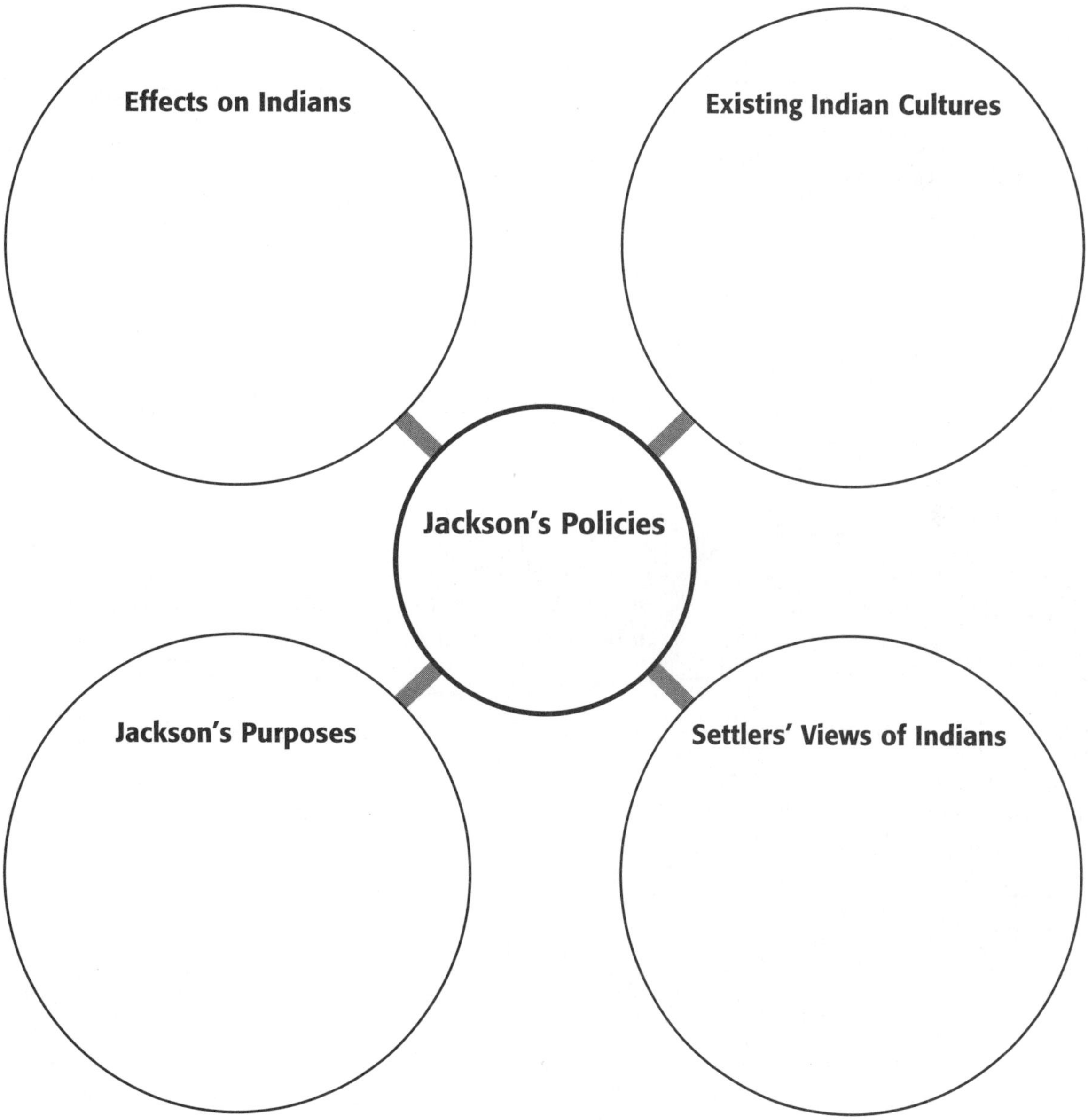

Effects on Indians

Existing Indian Cultures

Jackson's Policies

Jackson's Purposes

Settlers' Views of Indians

My opinion is: ____

____

____

Nationalism and Economic Growth

GRAPHIC ORGANIZER: POSSIBLE SOLUTION

Jackson's Indian Policies

Write your opinion of Jackson's Indian policies. Before writing, use the graphic organizer to collect facts and examples from your text.

Effects on Indians

Trail of Tears, thousands of deaths, Second Seminole War, loss of Indian homelands and culture

Existing Indian Cultures

Many groups gave up hunting and became farmers.

Cherokee farmers built towns;

Sequoya developed written Cherokee language;

Indians attempt to discuss and reason with Jackson.

Jackson's Policies

Indian Removal Act moves all tribes and nations to the West.

Jackson's Purposes

to build a strong nation of immigrants; to claim Indian territories for future immigrants and eventual American expansion

Settlers' Views of Indians

The settlers see Indians as competitors for land and as people who are easy to manipulate.

My opinion is: *Answers will vary and should include understanding of mistreatment and note facts from organizer to support ideas.*

Name ______________________ Class ____________ Date ____________

CHAPTER 8

Regional Societies

GRAPHIC ORGANIZER ACTIVITY

Arguments About Slavery

Under each heading on the graphic organizer, write the ideas expressed by each side and the reasons for their ideas.

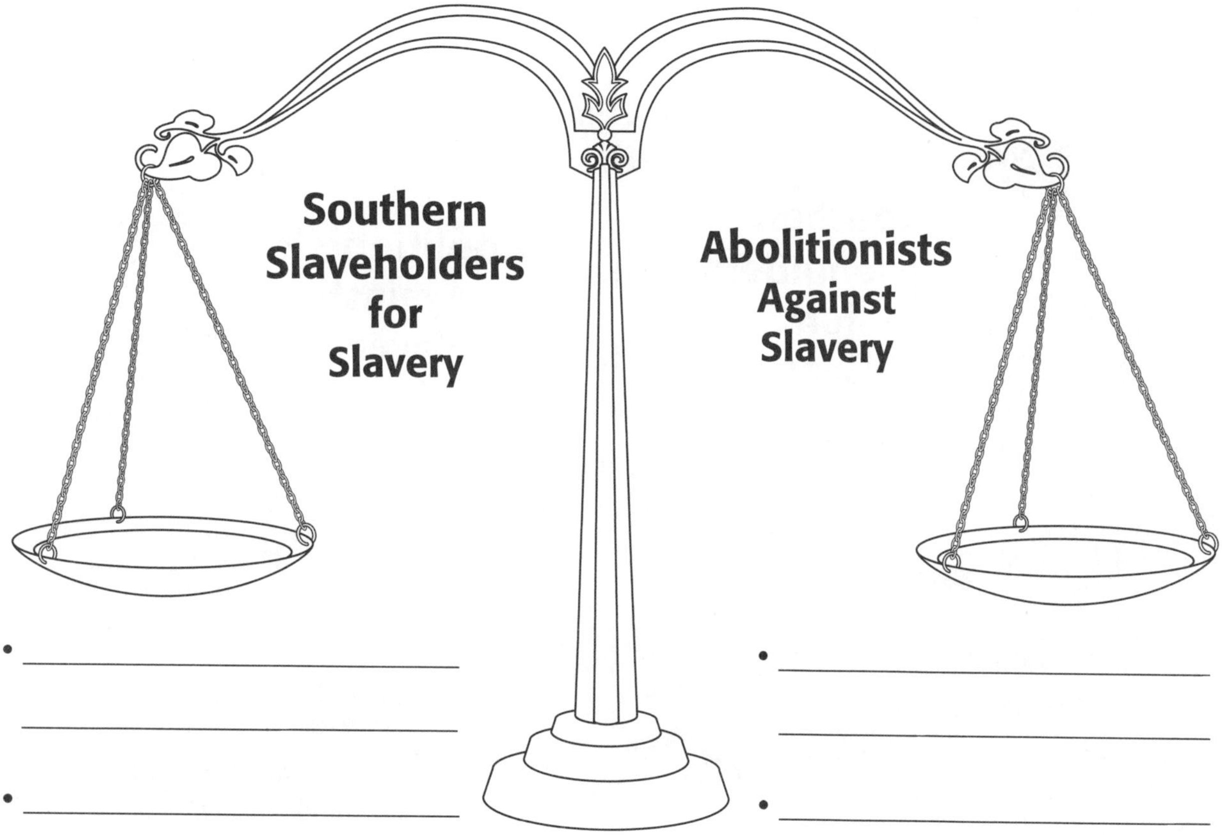

Southern Slaveholders for Slavery	Abolitionists Against Slavery
• ______________________	• ______________________
• ______________________	• ______________________
• ______________________	• ______________________

Regional Societies

GRAPHIC ORGANIZER: POSSIBLE SOLUTION

Arguments About Slavery

Under each heading on the graphic organizer, write the ideas expressed by each side and the reasons for their ideas.

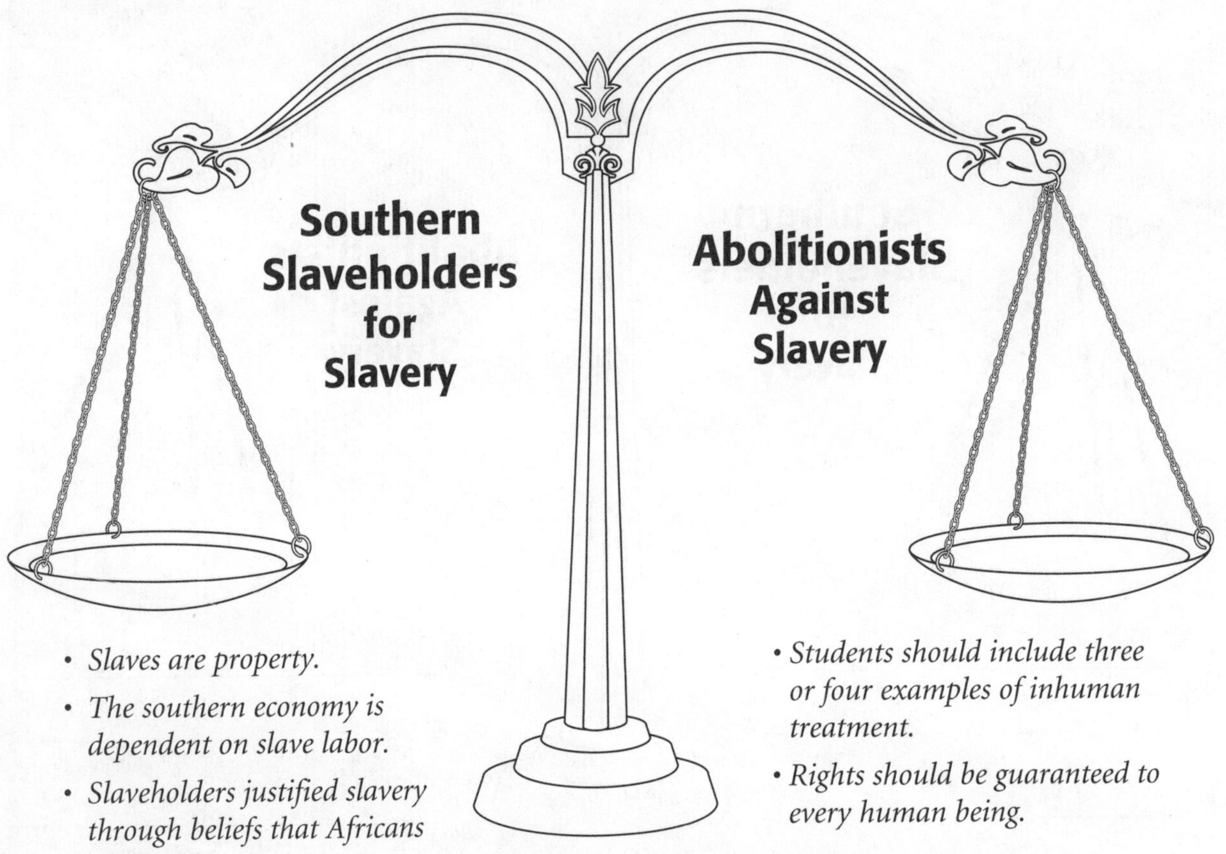

Southern Slaveholders for Slavery

- *Slaves are property.*
- *The southern economy is dependent on slave labor.*
- *Slaveholders justified slavery through beliefs that Africans were subhuman.*

Abolitionists Against Slavery

- *Students should include three or four examples of inhuman treatment.*
- *Rights should be guaranteed to every human being.*

Name ______________________ Class ____________ Date ____________

CHAPTER 9

Working for Reform

GRAPHIC ORGANIZER ACTIVITY

Women Working for a New America

Complete the graphic organizer by noting the accomplishments of each female leader.

S. and A. Grimké	Sojourner Truth	Mother Ann Lee
Dorothea Dix	Catharine Beecher	Emily Dickinson
Mary Jane Patterson	Susan B. Anthony	E. Cady Stanton & L. Mott
Emma Willard	Lucy Stone	Abby Kelley

Working for Reform

GRAPHIC ORGANIZER: POSSIBLE SOLUTION

Women Working for a New America

Complete the graphic organizer by noting the accomplishments of each female leader.

S. and A. Grimké

southern antislavery activists and Quakers; lectured and founded women's and antislavery organizations

Sojourner Truth

former slave; worked for American Anti-Slavery Society; preached abolition and women's rights

Mother Ann Lee

Shaker leader and founder; claimed to be the messiah; followers lived simply and did not marry

Dorothea Dix

reform for mental institutions; taught rehabilitation and humane treatment

Catharine Beecher

education reform; wrote and taught about the duty of women to teach morality to their husbands

Emily Dickinson

wrote poems reflecting romantic and transcendental views of nature

Mary Jane Patterson

first African American woman to receive a college degree in the United States

Susan B. Anthony

Quaker involved in temperance and abolition movements; helped pass Married Women's Property Act in New York; argued for women's right to enter law, medicine, and clergy

E. Cady Stanton & L. Mott

published Declaration of Sentiments; women's control of property, custody rights, and right to vote

Emma Willard

founded Troy Female Seminary, first college-level school for women, in 1821

Lucy Stone

influential speaker on women's movement; promoter of women's rights

Abby Kelley

member of American Anti-Slavery committee in 1840; active in women's movement

Name ______________________ Class ____________ Date ____________

Expansion and Conflict

GRAPHIC ORGANIZER ACTIVITY

Western Expansion

Fill in each column with facts about immigrants to the west.

	California	Oregon
Immigrants From		
Means of Travel		
Goals		
Hardships and Conflicts		
Rewards		

Expansion and Conflict

GRAPHIC ORGANIZER: POSSIBLE SOLUTION

Western Expansion

Fill in each column with facts about immigrants to the west.

	California	Oregon
Immigrants From	• *eastern United States, Europe, China*	• *eastern United States, the Midwest*
Means of Travel	• *overland on the California Trail* • *by sea to Central America, overland to the Pacific, then by ship to San Francisco*	• *most traveled overland by wagon train*
Goals	• *young unmarried men who wanted to strike it rich* • *Chinese who wanted to send money home*	• *families wanting new farms; to settle on new lands; build new communities*
Hardships and Conflicts	• *increased population fought and killed Indians* • *Chinese were prevented from staking claims* • *hardships of travel, starvation, scurvy, weather* • *many did not find gold* • *loneliness and wild cities*	• *Indians already lived on land: the Cayuse War* • *difficulties of travel, health, weather, rough roads*
Rewards	• *cultural diversity to California* • *some found gold and wealth* • *many remained in West* • *businesses flourished because of new wealth*	• *bountiful hunting and fishing* • *established new homes*

Name ______________________ Class __________ Date __________

Sectional Conflict Increases

GRAPHIC ORGANIZER ACTIVITY

The Lincoln-Douglas Debates

Complete the graphic organizer by listing points made by each senatorial candidate during the famous debates.

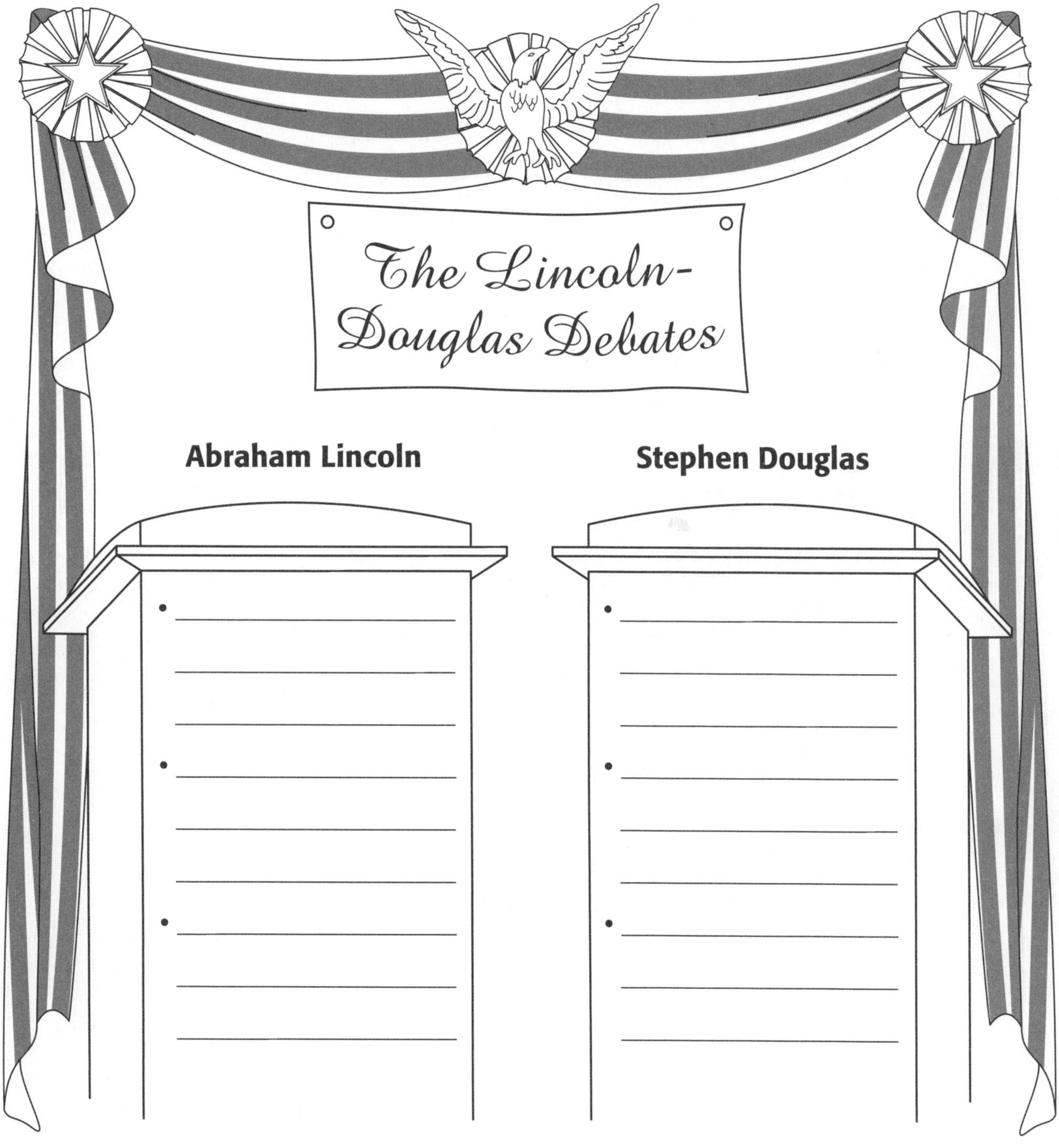

The Lincoln-Douglas Debates

Abraham Lincoln	Stephen Douglas
• ______________________	• ______________________
• ______________________	• ______________________
• ______________________	• ______________________

CHAPTER 11

Sectional Conflict Increases

GRAPHIC ORGANIZER: POSSIBLE SOLUTION

The Lincoln-Douglas Debates

Complete the graphic organizer by listing points made by each senatorial candidate during the famous debates.

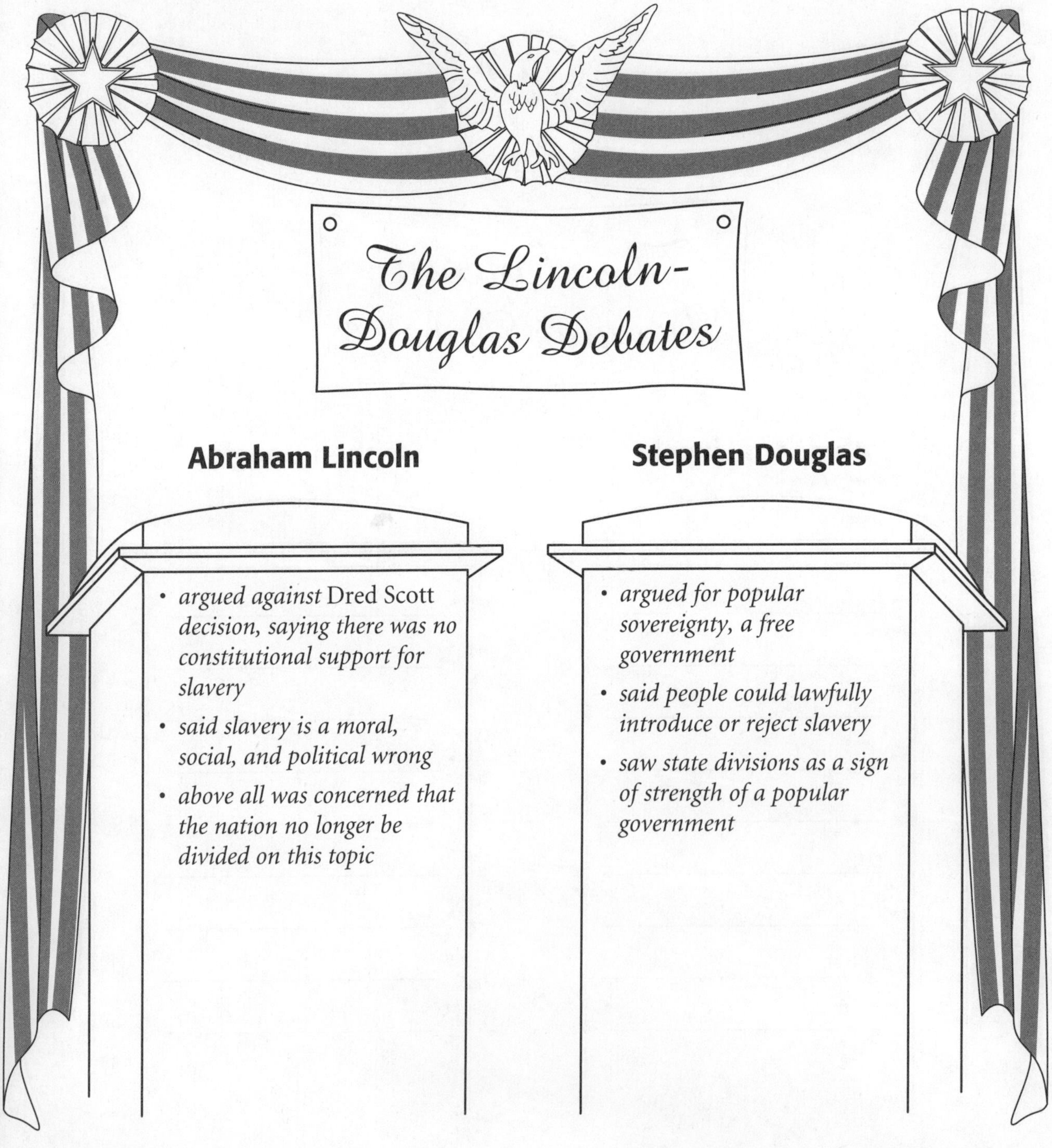
The Lincoln-Douglas Debates
Abraham Lincoln
• *argued against* Dred Scott *decision, saying there was no constitutional support for slavery*
• *said slavery is a moral, social, and political wrong*
• *above all was concerned that the nation no longer be divided on this topic*
Stephen Douglas
• *argued for popular sovereignty, a free government*
• *said people could lawfully introduce or reject slavery*
• *saw state divisions as a sign of strength of a popular government*

Name ______________________ Class ____________ Date ____________

CHAPTER 12

The Civil War

GRAPHIC ORGANIZER ACTIVITY

The Gettysburg Address

After reading the events of the Civil War, rewrite the Gettysburg Address, using your own words to express Lincoln's ideas. Before writing, use the graphic organizer to outline your ideas. Next to each circle is a statement describing one of the topics in the address. Reread the speech. Then, in each circle, explain what Lincoln meant by the topic statement.

(describe) the men who gave their lives

(details of) the struggle

Lincoln at Gettysburg

(describe) the unfinished work

(describe) the resolution

Now rewrite the Gettysburg Address in your own words.

____

____

____

____

____

____

____

____

The Civil War

GRAPHIC ORGANIZER: POSSIBLE SOLUTION

The Gettysburg Address

After reading the events of the Civil War, rewrite the Gettysburg Address, using your own words to express Lincoln's ideas. Before writing, use the graphic organizer to outline your ideas. Next to each circle is a statement describing one of the topics in the address. Reread the speech. Then, in each circle, explain what Lincoln meant by the topic statement.

Lincoln at Gettysburg

(describe) the men who gave their lives: *soldiers from both sides, young boys, farmers; people who believed fervently in succession or union*

(details of) the struggle: *a long bloody bat-tle; many soldiers killed; long days of marching and fighting off hunger, disease, fatigue*

(describe) the unfinished work: *to finish the war; to resolve the con-flict; to rebuild the country into one strong unified country*

(describe) the resolution: *to be sure there was a positive outcome that justified such a terrible loss*

Now rewrite the Gettysburg Address in your own words.

Answers may vary.

Name ____________ Class ________ Date ________

Reconstruction and the New South

GRAPHIC ORGANIZER ACTIVITY

Evaluating Reconstruction

Complete the graphic organizer by writing about the failure of Reconstruction to address problems of southern African Americans. Describe the problems and two leaders' conclusions about these problems.

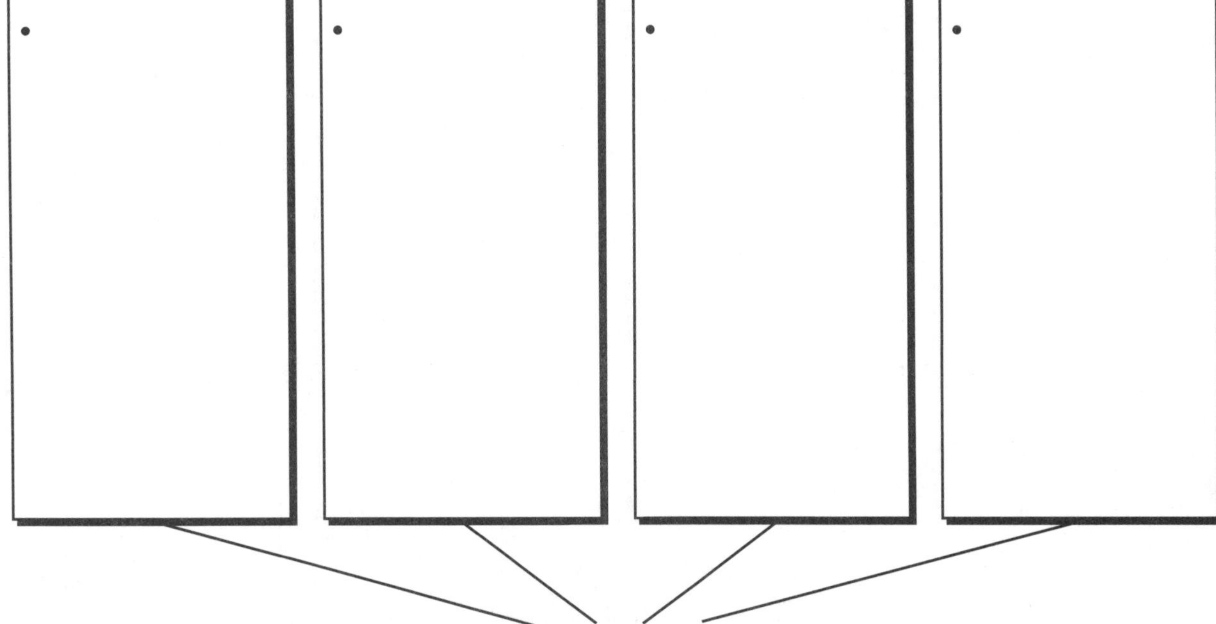

Ida B. Wells

Reconstruction and the New South

GRAPHIC ORGANIZER: POSSIBLE SOLUTION

Evaluating Reconstruction

Complete the graphic organizer by writing about the failure of Reconstruction to address problems of southern African Americans. Describe the problems and two leaders' conclusions about these problems.

Evidence of Shortcomings of Reconstruction

- *Sharecropping kept poor families in debt. Landowners often required them to raise only one crop, and raised prices on needed goods bought on credit.*

- *Poll taxes and literacy tests kept African Americans from voting. Actual physical danger or threat of it kept many African Americans from the polls.*

- *Courts ruled segregation legal. Jim Crow laws went into effect. Segregation provided an excuse for delivering substandard services to African Americans.*

- *KKK activities threatened all aspects of life. White citizens threatened, attacked, and lynched African Americans, causing fearful situations.*

Conclusions

Booker T. Washington

African Americans should develop skills in trades and professions because economic independence was the key to political and social equality.

Ida B. Wells

African Americans should focus on protesting unfair treatment and especially lynching. If this failed, she urged African Americans to leave the South.

Name ______________ Class ______ Date ______

CHAPTER 14

The Western Crossroads

GRAPHIC ORGANIZER ACTIVITY

American Indian Leaders

To complete the graphic organizer, note the actions and words of each American Indian leader, along with reasons and examples for each leader's approach.

Chief Joseph

Nation:

Actions:

In his own words:

Wovoka

Nation:

Actions:

In his own words:

Geronimo

Nation:

Actions:

In his own words:

Sitting Bull

Nation:

Actions:

In his own words:

The Western Crossroads

GRAPHIC ORGANIZER: POSSIBLE SOLUTION

American Indian Leaders

To complete the graphic organizer, note the actions and words of each American Indian leader, along with reasons and examples for each leader's approach.

Chief Joseph

Nation: *Nez Percé*

Actions: *The Nez Percé killed four white settlers in revenge for losing their homeland; they were chased to Canada, and eventually surrendered. The Nez Percé were removed from their homelands. Chief Joseph was sent to Washington.*

In his own words: *"I am tired of fighting. Our chiefs are killed. . . . It is cold and we have no blankets. The little children are freezing to death. . . .My heart is sick and sad. From where the sun now stands, I will fight no more forever."*

Wovoka

Nation: *Paiute*

Actions: *He began a religious movement known as the Ghost Dance.*

In his own words: *He said that the white settlers would vanish, dead Indian ancestors would return to life, and the buffalo and traditional Indian ways would return.*

Geronimo

Nation: *Apache*

Actions: *When the government forced the Apache to resettle in a reservation, Geronimo and 75 followers fled the army for five years.*

In his own words: *"Once I moved about like the wind. Now I surrender to you and that is all."*

Sitting Bull

Nation: *Sioux*

Actions: *He resisted the U.S. government's claims to his land and fought the Battle of Little Bighorn, defeating Custer. Eventually, he was forced to surrender, fled to Canada, and returned. Later he was killed in a skirmish on a reservation.*

In his own words: *"You are fools to make yourselves slaves to a piece of fat bacon, some hard-tack, and a little sugar and coffee."*

Name ______________________ Class ___________ Date ___________

CHAPTER 15

The Second Industrial Revolution

GRAPHIC ORGANIZER ACTIVITY

Industry Problems in the Late 1800s

Complete the Problem/Solution chart by explaining how each problem was solved.

Problem		Solution
Large monopolies had no obligation to keep prices low or maintain quality.	How did the federal government solve this problem? →	
Poor immigrant and African American families did not make a living wage.	How did families try to solve this problem? →	
Children worked 12-hour shifts for pennies a day; workers were exhausted and sometimes died from careless accidents; employers did not improve safety.	How did workers try to solve this problem? →	
Union activists riot.	How did employers solve this problem? →	

The Second Industrial Revolution

GRAPHIC ORGANIZER: POSSIBLE SOLUTION

Industry Problems in the Late 1800s

Complete the Problem/Solution chart by explaining how each problem was solved.

Problem		Solution
Large monopolies had no obligation to keep prices low or maintain quality.	How did the federal government solve this problem? →	*Sherman Antitrust Act outlawed monopolies and trusts that restrained trade.*
Poor immigrant and African American families did not make a living wage.	How did families try to solve this problem? →	*Women and children in many families worked long hours.*
Children worked 12-hour shifts for pennies a day; workers were exhausted and sometimes died from careless accidents; employers did not improve safety.	How did workers try to solve this problem? →	*The Knights of Labor was formed, began organizing labor unions.*
Union activists riot.	How did employers solve this problem? →	*They required workers to sign pledges against unions, blacklisted union members; they locked out union members and hired strikebreakers.*

Name ______________________ Class ____________ Date ____________

The Transformation of American Society

GRAPHIC ORGANIZER ACTIVITY

Daily Life in the Cities

Study the outline below. Then complete the graphic organizer by outlining Section 3, Daily Life in the Cities.

I. Education
   A. Social reformers worked to expand education for children.
      1. compulsory education laws; public schools
      2. ______________________
      3. ______________________
   B. Opportunities were not equal for everyone.
      1. ______________________
      2. ______________________
      3. ______________________
II. Publishing
   A. ______________________
   B. ______________________
      1. Printers developed better methods, and newspaper circulation grew rapidly.
      2. Literature became more popular.
         a. ______________________
         b. ______________________
         c. ______________________
III. Leisure Time in Urban Parks
   A. Planners developed huge urban parks.
   B. ______________________
   C. ______________________
IV. Leisure and Sports
   A. Baseball grew as a participatory and spectator sport.
      1. ______________________
      2. ______________________
      3. ______________________
      4. ______________________
   B. Football became more popular.
      1. ______________________
      2. ______________________
   C. Basketball was invented as a winter game.
      1. ______________________
      2. ______________________
V. Entertainment
   A. People came to the cities for entertainment.
      1. ______________________
      2. ______________________
   B. Ragtime became popular.
      1. ______________________
      2. ______________________

The Transformation of American Society

GRAPHIC ORGANIZER: POSSIBLE SOLUTION

Daily Life in the Cities

Study the outline below. Then complete the graphic organizer by outlining Section 3, Daily Life in the Cities.

I. Education
  A. Social reformers worked to expand education for children.
    1. compulsory education laws; public schools
    2. *John Dewey stressed cooperative learning and emphasized art, history, science*
    3. *Harris and Cubberley believed in teaching behavior, loyalty, and values.*
  B. Opportunities were not equal for everyone.
    1. *Segregation created low-quality education for nonwhites.*
    2. *Opportunities rose for women.*
    3. *College enrollment expanded, primarily for wealthy and upper-middle class.*

II. Publishing
  A. *By 1900, 90 percent of Americans could read.*
  B. *Printed media became the primary information source for urban populations.*
    1. Printers developed better methods, and newspaper circulation grew rapidly.
    2. Literature became more popular.
      a. *adventure stories*
      b. *realistic novels and stories*
      c. *Christian novels*

III. Leisure Time in Urban Parks
  A. Planners developed huge urban parks.
  B. *Frederick Law Olmstead designed Central Park.*
  C. *The City Beautiful movement stressed parks and attractive streets.*

IV. Leisure and Sports
  A. Baseball grew as a participatory and spectator sport.
    1. *In 1869 Aaron Champion organized the first professional baseball team.*
    2. *William Hulbert organized the National League in 1876.*
    3. *the first World Series*
    4. *African Americans banned from professional teams*
  B. Football became more popular.
    1. *Walter Camp made contributions to the structure of the sport.*
    2. *Congress discussed banning it, due to the violent nature of the sport.*
  C. Basketball was invented as a winter game.
    1. *James Naismith invented the game in 1891.*
    2. *Colleges created both male and female teams.*

V. Entertainment
  A. People came to the cities for entertainment.
    1. *Edwin Booth popularized Shakespeare.*
    2. *Vaudeville shows included animal acts, comedy, musicians, and skits.*
  B. Ragtime became popular.
    1. *Scott Joplin's "Maple Leaf Rag" became popular.*
    2. *New dances like the Cakewalk and Turkey Trot became popular.*

Name ______________________ Class ____________ Date ____________

Politics in the Gilded Age

GRAPHIC ORGANIZER ACTIVITY

An Expanding Population

The chart below presents U.S. population by residence. Using this information, chart the growth of the U.S. population from 1790 to the early 1900s.

Year	Urban	Rural
1790	202	3,728
1800	[no data]	[no data]
1810	525	6,714
1820	693	8,945
1830	[no data]	[no data]
1840	1,845	15,224
1850	[no data]	[no data]
1860	6,217	25,227
1870	9,902	28,656
1880	14,130	36,026
1890	22,106	40,841
1900	30,160	45,835
1910	[no data]	[no data]
1920	54,158	51,553

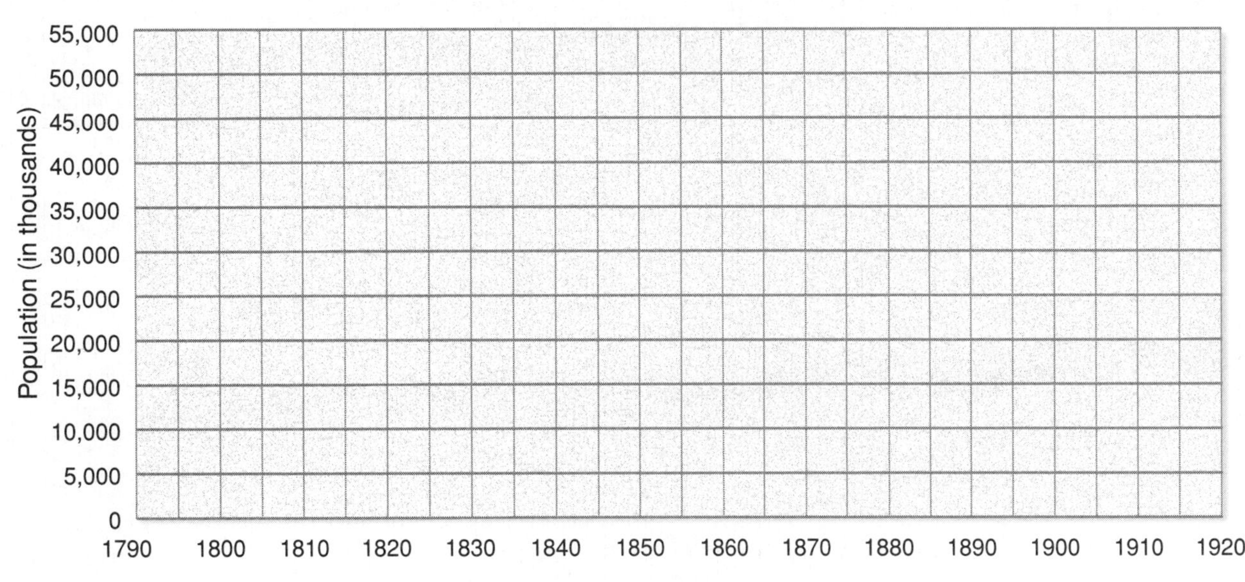

Politics in the Gilded Age

GRAPHIC ORGANIZER: POSSIBLE SOLUTION

An Expanding Population

The chart below presents U.S. population by residence. Using this information, chart the growth of the U.S. population from 1790 to the early 1900s.

Year	Urban	Rural
1790	202	3,728
1800	[no data]	[no data]
1810	525	6,714
1820	693	8,945
1830	[no data]	[no data]
1840	1,845	15,224
1850	[no data]	[no data]
1860	6,217	25,227
1870	9,902	28,656
1880	14,130	36,026
1890	22,106	40,841
1900	30,160	45,835
1910	[no data]	[no data]
1920	54,158	51,553

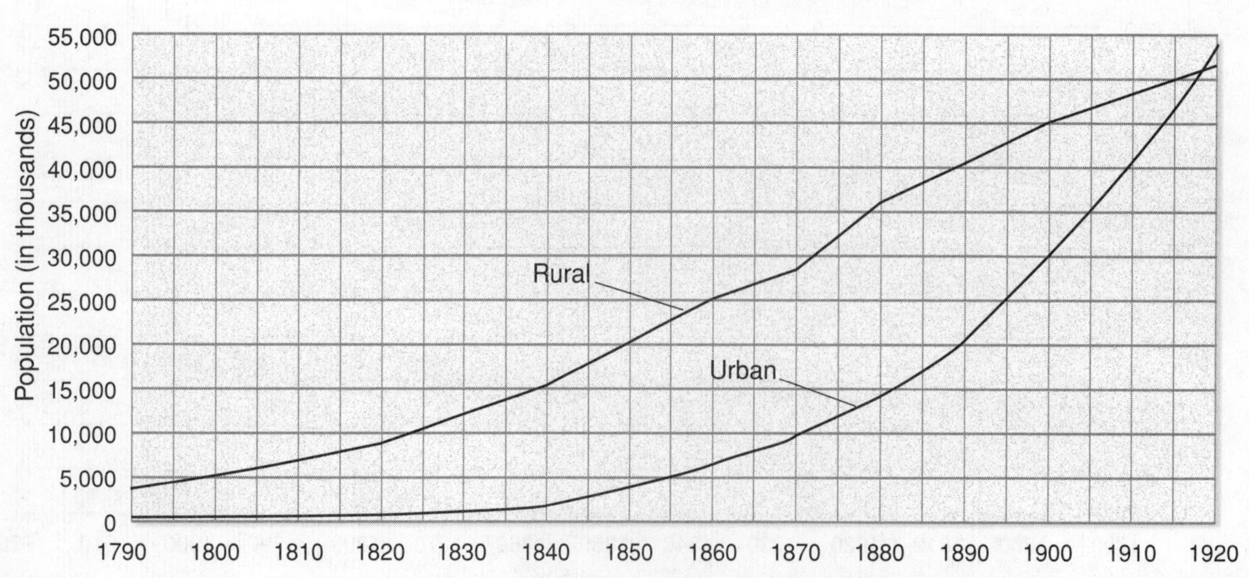

Name ________________ Class ________ Date ________

The Age of Reform

GRAPHIC ORGANIZER ACTIVITY

The Progressive Ideal

Create protest signs that support the statement at the bottom of the page. Then write a brief statement explaining why a critic made this comment in the early 1900s.

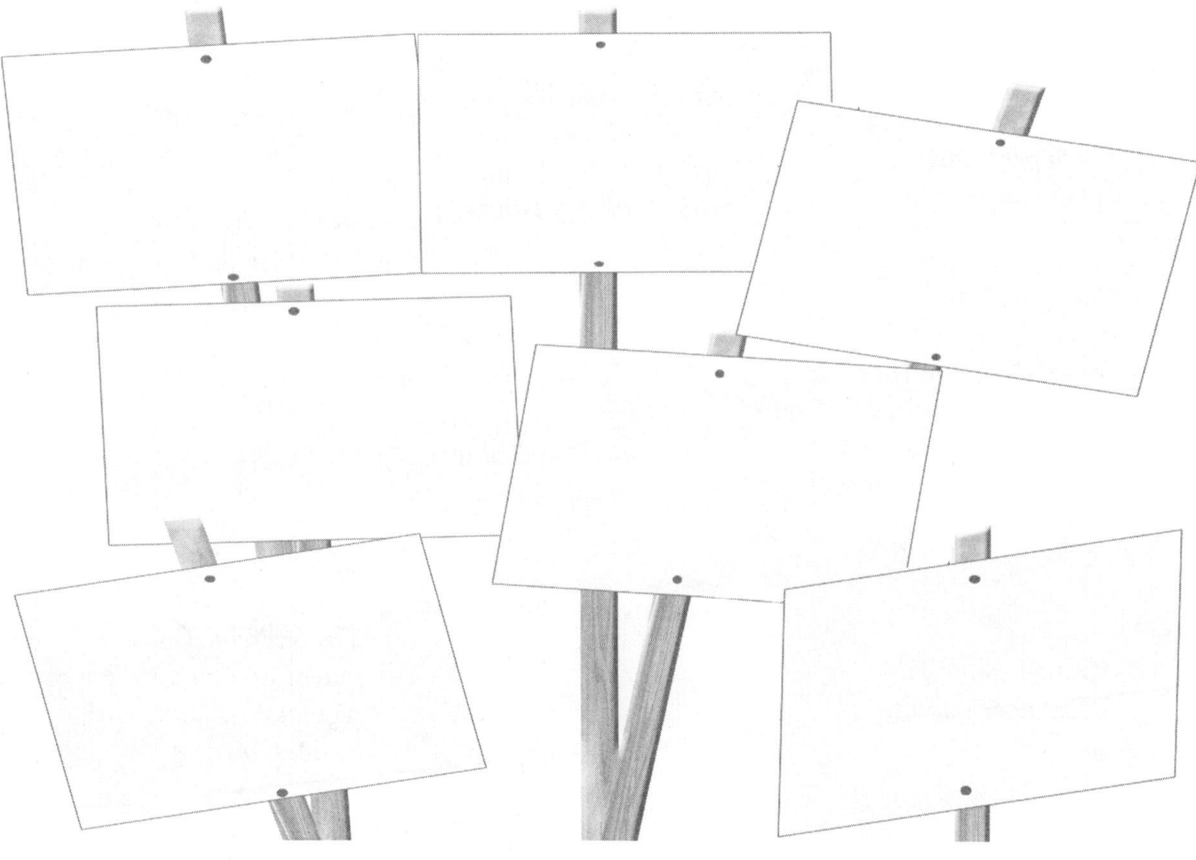

Capital has neither morals nor ideals.

The Age of Reform

GRAPHIC ORGANIZER: POSSIBLE SOLUTION

The Progressive Ideal

Create protest signs that support the statement at the bottom of the page. Then write a brief statement explaining why a critic made this comment in the early 1900s.

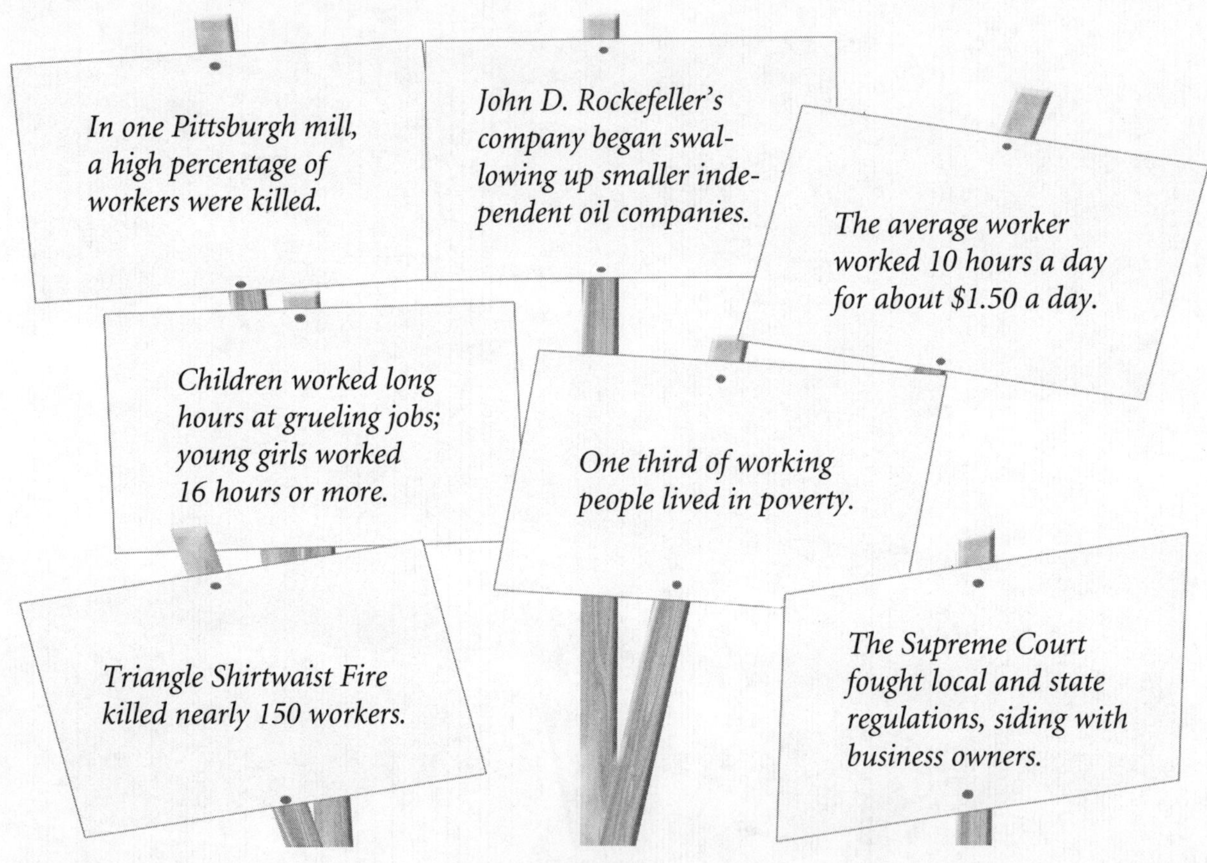

Capital has neither morals nor ideals.

Answers will vary but should address the fact that employers exploited workers, had little regard for life or quality of life, and were primarily interested in profit.

Name ______________________ Class ____________ Date ____________

CHAPTER 19

Progressive Politicians

GRAPHIC ORGANIZER ACTIVITY

Women's Suffrage

Complete the graphic organizer by writing a letter from the perspective of a woman between 1918 and 1920. Compose a letter to one of the senators who voted against suffrage in 1918. List reasons and examples, including obvious inequities between men and women, and explain reforms you would vote for if you had the right.

____

Dear ______________________

____

____

____

____

____

____

____

____

____

____

____

____

Sincerely,

____

Progressive Politicians

GRAPHIC ORGANIZER: POSSIBLE SOLUTION

Women's Suffrage

Complete the graphic organizer by writing a letter from the perspective of a woman between 1918 and 1920. Compose a letter to one of the senators who voted against suffrage in 1918. List reasons and examples, including obvious inequities between men and women, and explain reforms you would vote for if you had the right.

Dear ____________

Text of letter will vary but should address the fact that women showed support and patriotism during the war and deserve to participate in the decision-making process. Suggestions for reforms might include concerns over education, child labor, and labor in general.

Sincerely,

____

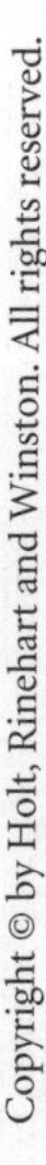

Name ____________________ Class __________ Date __________

CHAPTER 20

America and the World

GRAPHIC ORGANIZER ACTIVITY

Changes in Cuba

Complete the time line with events centered around Cuban independence.

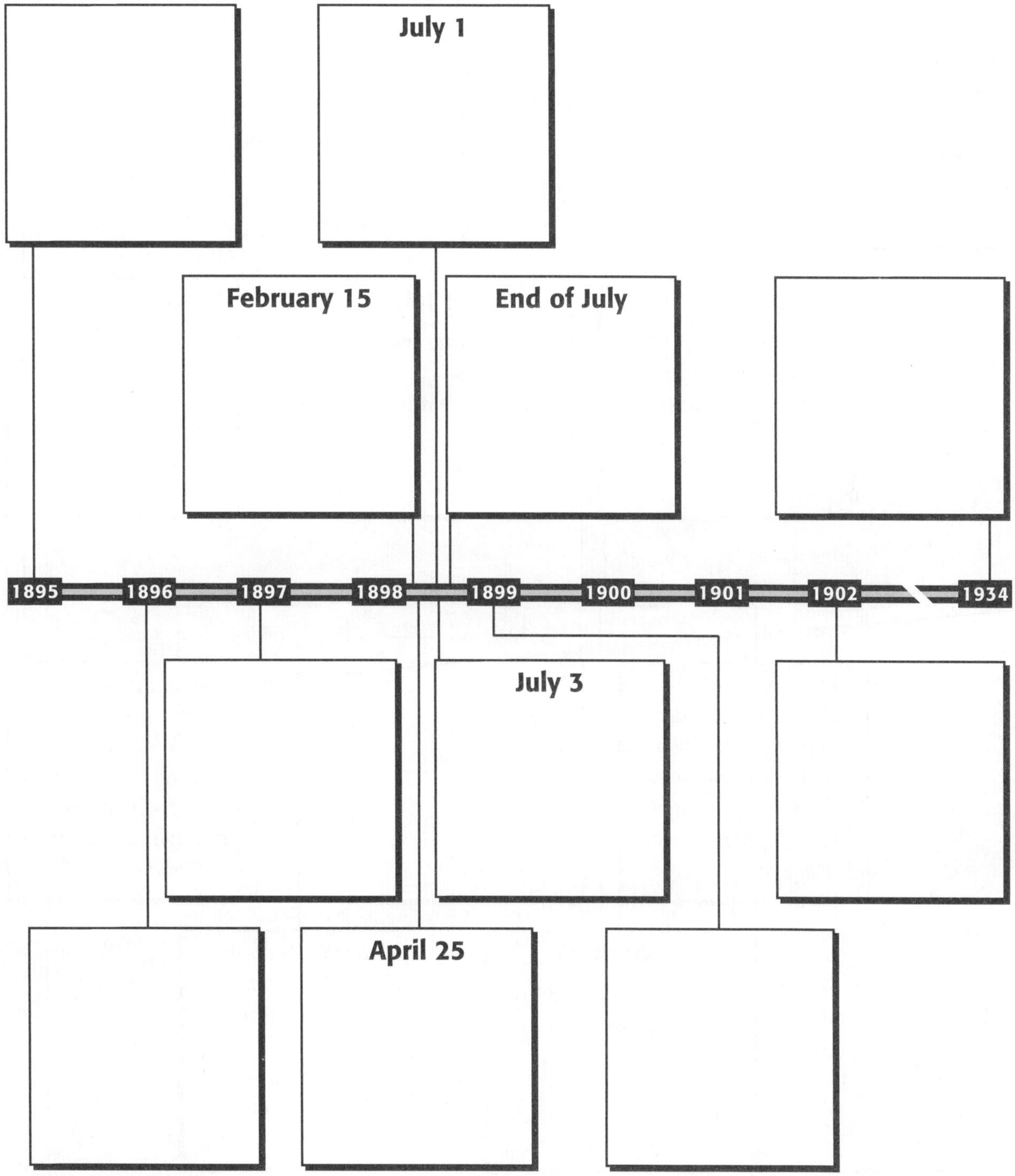
July 1
February 15
End of July
1895
1896
1897
1898
1899
1900
1901
1902
1934
July 3
April 25

America and the World

GRAPHIC ORGANIZER: POSSIBLE SOLUTION

Changes in Cuba

Complete the time line with events centered around Cuban independence.

1895

José Martí joins Cuban revolutionaries and becomes a martyr for the independence movement.

1896

General Valeriano Weyler arrives from Spain to put down uprisings; he imprisons many farmers.

1897

William Randolph Hearst sends Frederic Remington to Cuba to create drawings showing Spanish cruelty to boost support for war with Spain.

1898

February 15
The battleship USS Maine *blows up, killing 260 sailors.*

April 25
Congress declares war on Spain.

July 1
United States attacks Santiago.

July 3
United States sinks the Spanish fleet.

End of July
United States wins the Spanish-American War.

1899

McKinley appoints General Leonard Wood as governor of Cuba. Wood organizes schools and a sanitation system.

1900

1901

1902

Cuba reluctantly accepts the Platt Amendment, giving U.S. responsibility to protect Cuba and the right to intervene in Cuba's affairs.

1934

United States renounces right to intervene in Cuba.

CHAPTER 21

World War I

GRAPHIC ORGANIZER ACTIVITY

Americans in World War I

Complete the graphic organizer by comparing and contrasting aspects of life for Americans abroad and at home during World War I.

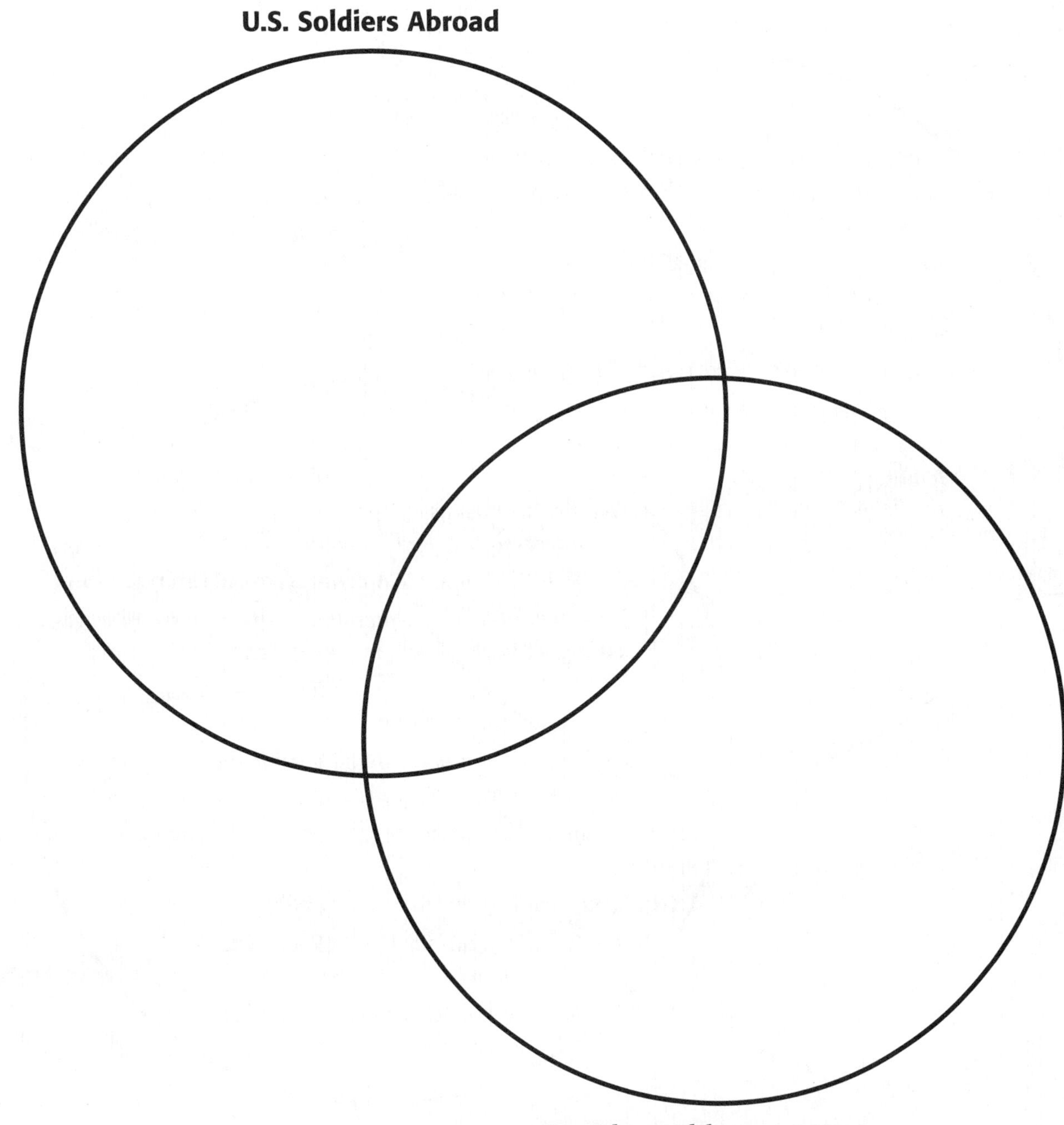

World War I

GRAPHIC ORGANIZER: POSSIBLE SOLUTION

Americans in World War I

Complete the graphic organizer by comparing and contrasting aspects of life for Americans abroad and at home during World War I.

U.S. Soldiers Abroad

Men faced new weapons, such as machine guns, tanks, poison gas, submarines, and airplanes.

Men had honed fighting skills but were unprepared for the long treks, exhaustion, and danger.

African Americans were discriminated against.

Women worked in hospitals for 18 hours straight, tending patients off the fields.

Answers will vary but should include some of the following points:

Women worked as volunteers for the Red Cross and YMCA.

Americans had strong sense of purpose.

Americans were asked to reduce food consumption by observing wheatless and meatless days.

Americans created victory gardens.

Rates and limits were set on wages and interest rates.

Working conditions improved when needed workers went on strike.

More women worked outside the home; 1.5 million women worked in industry.

Americans joined the volunteer effort, conserved energy, recycled materials.

Girl Scouts worked toward the war effort.

In the Great Migration, 1915–1930, African Americans moved to the North.

Quakers and Mennonites opposed the war.

The Socialist Party opposed the war.

American Citizens at Home

CHAPTER 22

A Turbulent Decade

GRAPHIC ORGANIZER ACTIVITY

Postwar Conflicts

Read the information and questions on the graphic organizer. Then write the cause or effect in each empty box.

Cause		Effect
	What was the cause of the sudden change? ←	Demand for jobs was high; unemployment rose; wages fell.
	What was the cause of this displacement? ←	Women were displaced from the workplace.
U.S. government cancels more than $2 billion in defense contracts.	What was the effect on the job market? →	
European farm production revives after the war.	How did this affect American farmers? →	
	What were several causes of these fears? ←	Fears of revolution rose, giving rise to anticommunist hysteria.
Postal clerks discover 36 bombs addressed to prominent citizens.	What was the government's response to this event? →	

A Turbulent Decade

GRAPHIC ORGANIZER: POSSIBLE SOLUTION

Postwar Conflicts

Read the information and questions on the graphic organizer. Then write the cause or effect in each empty box.

Cause		Effect
4.5 million soldiers returned from the war.	What was the cause of the sudden change? ←	Demand for jobs was high; unemployment rose; wages fell.
Veterans wanted their jobs back.	What was the cause of this displacement? ←	Women were displaced from the workplace.
U.S. government cancels more than $2 billion in defense contracts.	What was the effect on the job market? →	*many cutbacks; layoffs; lower wages*
European farm production revives after the war.	How did this affect American farmers? →	*Prices fall in United States and farmers lose money, leading to a farm crisis.*
a series of strikes: Seattle general strike; Boston police strike; United Mine Workers strike; Russian Revolution in 1917	What were several causes of these fears? ←	Fears of revolution rose, giving rise to anticommunist hysteria.
Postal clerks discover 36 bombs addressed to prominent citizens.	What was the government's response to this event? →	*Palmer's anticommunist crusade; the Palmer raids; federal officials arrest thousands*

Name ____________________ Class __________ Date __________

CHAPTER 23

The Jazz Age

GRAPHIC ORGANIZER ACTIVITY

Artists of the 1920s and 1930s

Complete the graphic organizer by listing artists in each field. Briefly describe each person's artistic contribution to American culture.

The Creative Era

Music	Literature	Art and Architecture
•	•	•
•	•	•
•	•	•
•	•	•
•	•	•
	•	•
	•	•
		•

Research one person in each category. Write two or three sentences describing each person's contribution to culture in the early 1900s.

Music ____

____

Literature ____

____

Art or Architecture ____

____

The Jazz Age

GRAPHIC ORGANIZER: POSSIBLE SOLUTION

Artists of the 1920s and 1930s

Complete the graphic organizer by listing artists in each field. Briefly describe each person's artistic contribution to American culture.

The Creative Era

Music	Literature	Art and Architecture
• *Bessie Smith, jazz and blues singer* • *Jelly Roll Morton, jazz pianist* • *Louis Armstrong, jazz trumpeter and singer* • *Duke Ellington, jazz composer and orchestra leader* • *Paul Robeson, actor and singer*	• *Langston Hughes, poet* • *James Weldon Johnson, poet and novelist* • *Ernest Hemingway, novelist* • *Sinclair Lewis, novelist* • *Henry L. Mencken, journalist* • *F. Scott Fitzgerald, novelist* • *Eugene O'Neill, playwright*	• *Edward Hopper, painter* • *Alfred Steiglitz, photographer and gallery owner* • *José Clemente Orozco, mural painter* • *David Alfaro Siquieros, mural painter* • *Diego Rivera, mural painter* • *Frida Kahlo, painter* • *Frank Lloyd Wright, architect* • *Louis Sullivan, architect*

Research one person in each category. Write two or three sentences describing each person's contribution to culture in the early 1900s.

Music *Answers will vary and should include details of the themes, ideas, and contributions of three artists.*

____

Literature ____

____

Art or Architecture ____

____

Name ______________________ Class __________ Date __________

CHAPTER 24

The Great Depression

GRAPHIC ORGANIZER ACTIVITY

Life During the Depression

Complete the graphic organizer by writing a letter about the Great Depression. Write as if you are telling a younger family member what it was like when you grew up during the 1930s. In your letter, answer the following questions:

- What did your family lose when the stock market crashed?
- How did members of your family respond to the loss?
- What was your daily life like?
- What hardships did people suffer in your city or town?
- Which organizations helped you or people you know?

____

Dear ______________________

____

____

____

____

____

____

____

____

____

Sincerely,

____

CHAPTER 24

The Great Depression

GRAPHIC ORGANIZER: POSSIBLE SOLUTION

Life During the Depression

Complete the graphic organizer by writing a letter about the Great Depression. Write as if you are telling a younger family member what it was like when you grew up during the 1930s. In your letter, answer the following questions:

- What did your family lose when the stock market crashed?
- How did members of your family respond to the loss?
- What was your daily life like?
- What hardships did people suffer in your city or town?
- Which organizations helped you or people you know?

Dear ______________

Letters will vary and should include answers to the above questions and an indication of the hardships visited on families and effect on most people in a community. Students should include examples from the text.

Sincerely,

____

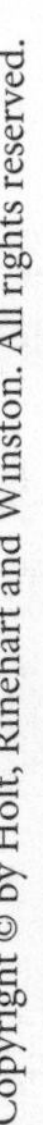

Name ______________________ Class ____________ Date ____________

CHAPTER 25

The New Deal

GRAPHIC ORGANIZER ACTIVITY

Social Change in the 1930s

Think of yourself as an artist from the 1930s. Write or draw your idea for a piece of artwork that reflects your experience and the experience of other Americans. You may write an outline for a story or play, design an oral history project, or illustrate the lives of people around you. Use information from your text for guidance.

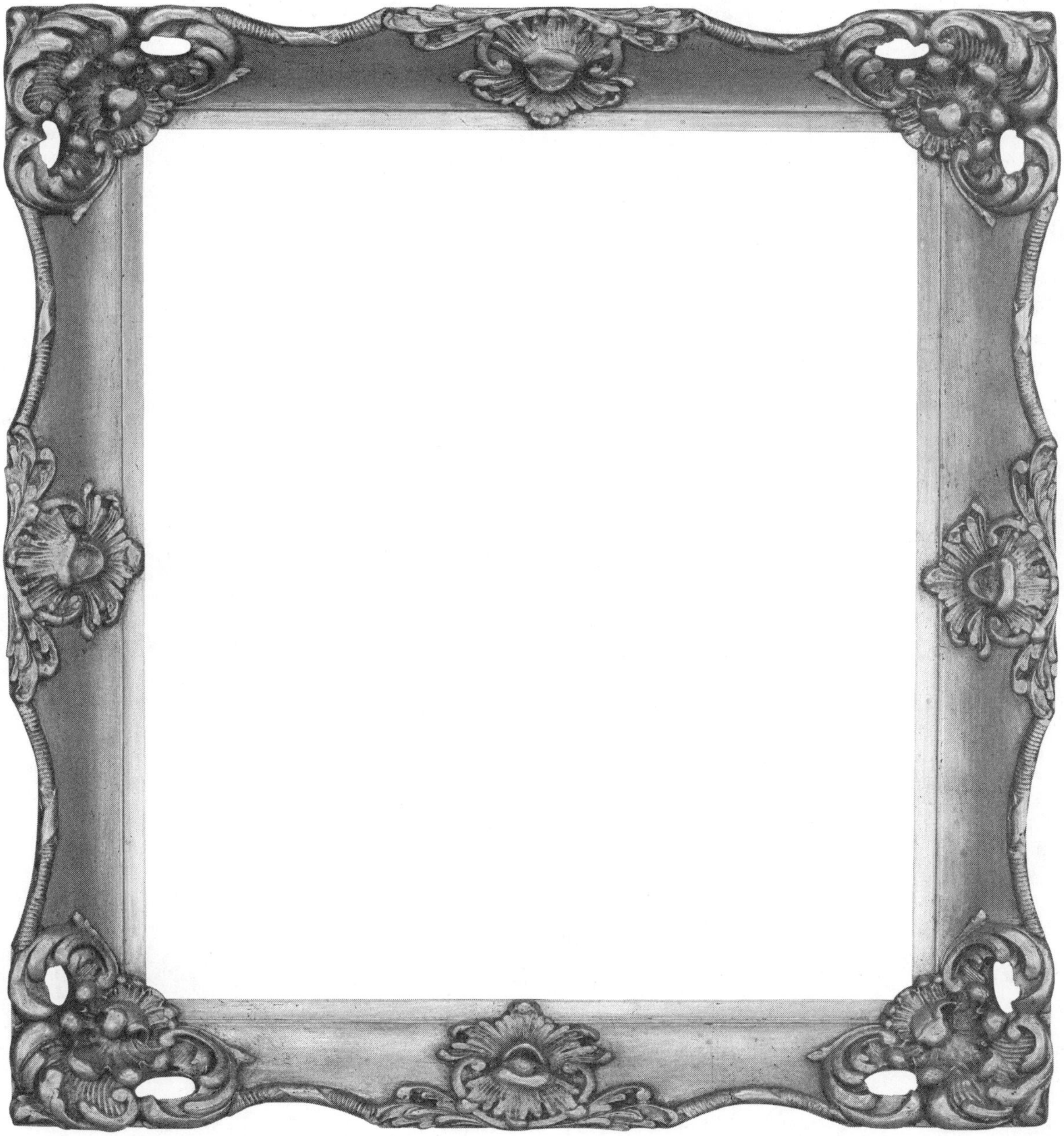

Title of Work ______________________________________

The New Deal

GRAPHIC ORGANIZER: POSSIBLE SOLUTION

Social Change in the 1930s

Think of yourself as an artist from the 1930s. Write or draw your idea for a piece of artwork that reflects your experience and the experience of other Americans. You may write an outline for a story or play, design an oral history project, or illustrate the lives of people around you. Use information from your text for guidance.

Answers will vary greatly and should indicate an understanding of social change in the 1930s.

Title of Work ____

Name ________________ Class ________ Date ________

CHAPTER 26

The Road to War

GRAPHIC ORGANIZER ACTIVITY

A Shift in International Relations

Complete the chart by describing the relationship between each pair of countries early in World War II (1939–1941).

At the beginning of World War II, what was the relationship between . . . ?

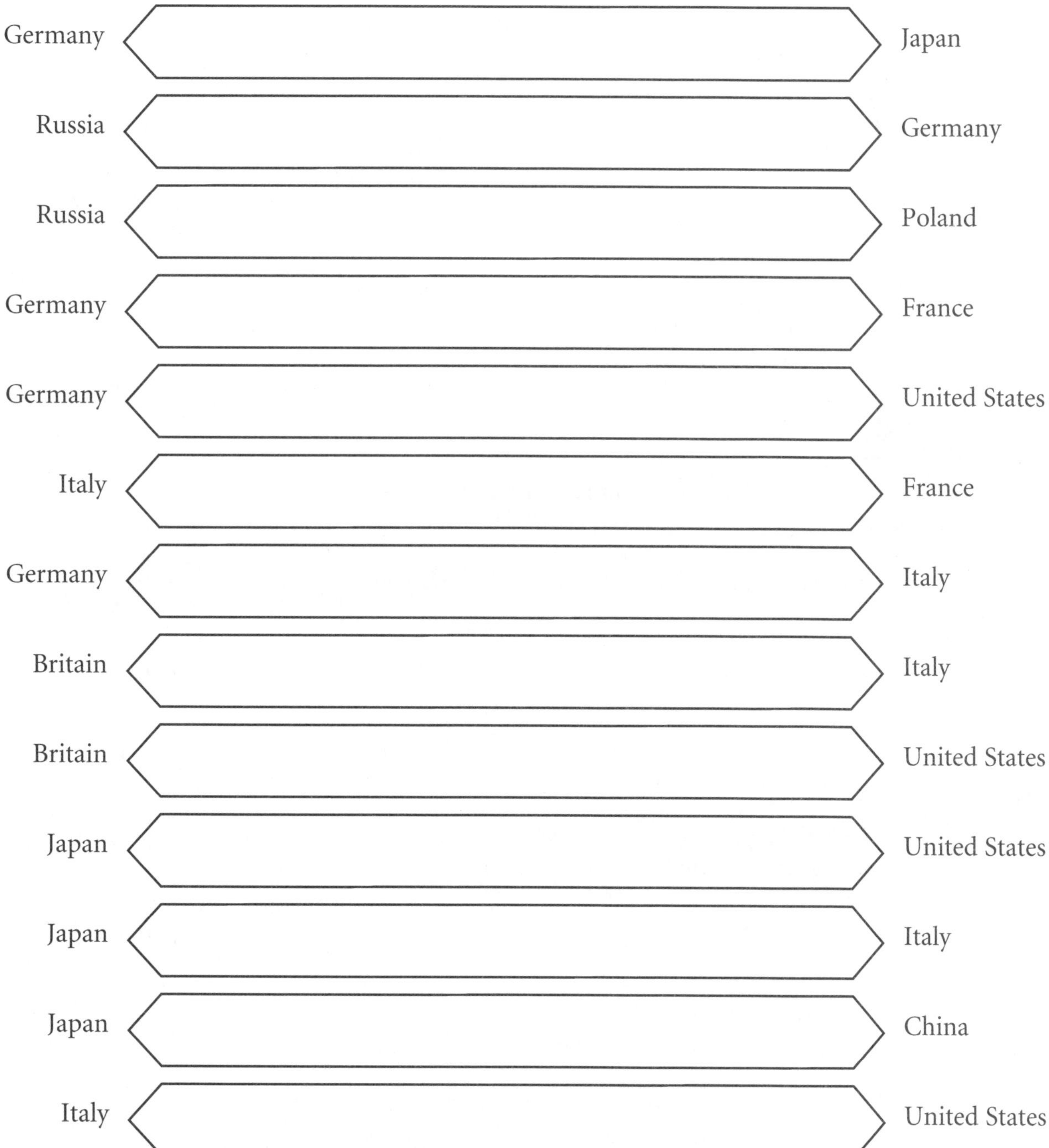

The Road to War

GRAPHIC ORGANIZER: POSSIBLE SOLUTION

A Shift in International Relations

Complete the chart by describing the relationship between each pair of countries early in World War II (1939–1941).

At the beginning of World War II, what was the relationship between . . . ?

Germany	*both used military strength to expand control; eventually joined forces as Axis Powers*	Japan
Russia	*Stalin signed a nonaggression pact with Germany, 1939.*	Germany
Russia	*joined Germany in an invasion of Poland*	Poland
Germany	*When Hitler bombed Poland, France joined the war. Germany invaded France in 1940.*	France
Germany	*U.S. warships began to patrol the Atlantic in 1941, looking for Italian and German submarines.*	United States
Italy	*Italy declared war on Britain and France in 1940.*	France
Germany	*formed a military alliance known as the Axis Powers*	Italy
Britain	*Italy declared war on Britain and France in 1940.*	Italy
Britain	*The United States implemented a lend-lease act to provide Britain with military supplies.*	United States
Japan	*The United States froze all Japanese assets and implemented an embargo on U.S. imports. Japan bombed Pearl Harbor in 1941.*	United States
Japan	*Japan joined the Axis military powers of Italy and Germany.*	Italy
Japan	*Japan wanted to expand its military control throughout Asia; invaded Manchuria and Nanking.*	China
Italy	*The United States banned shipments to Italy in protest about Ethiopia, then assisted the Allies with weapons and warships in the Atlantic.*	United States

Name ______________________ Class __________ Date __________

CHAPTER 27

Americans in World War II

GRAPHIC ORGANIZER ACTIVITY

The Effect of War on Life at Home

Waging war requires sacrifices and life style changes from everyone, including people living at home. Use the graphic organizers below to spell out such war-time changes.

The Effect of World War II on Life at Home

Home Life

1. ______________________

____

2. ______________________

____

Music and Movies

1. ______________________

____

2. ______________________

____

Labor

1. ______________________

____

2. ______________________

____

Literature

1. ______________________

____

2. ______________________

____

Americans in World War II

GRAPHIC ORGANIZER: POSSIBLE SOLUTION

The Effect of War on Life at Home

Waging war requires sacrifices and life style changes from everyone, including people living at home. Use the graphic organizers below to spell out such war-time changes.

Answers will vary but may include some of the following.

The Effect of World War II on Life at Home

Home Life

Families cut back on consumption of both luxuries and necessities; kept victory gardens; canned own food; had nighttime blackouts.

Music and Movies

Movie stars sold war bonds and entertained troops; movies told war stories; music captured the harsh reality of the war; "God Bless America" became the unofficial national anthem.

Labor

Women replaced men that had gone off to war in jobs at all levels; blacks and other minorities moved into better jobs but faced discrimination; discrimination led to laws banning it on work done for war contracts.

Literature

Nonfiction books became more popular than works of fiction; paperback books arose in response to rationing and distribution to soldiers overseas.

Name ______________________ Class ____________ Date ____________

CHAPTER 28

The Cold War

GRAPHIC ORGANIZER ACTIVITY

U.S. Presence in Global Affairs

Complete the chart by writing several sentences to describe each organization. Explain how and why the United States is involved in international affairs.

U.S. Involvement in International Affairs

	Who?	What?	How it solves problems?	Why?
United Nations (UN)				
North Atlantic Treaty Organization (NATO)				
Central Intelligence Agency (CIA)				
National Security Council (NSC)				

The Cold War

GRAPHIC ORGANIZER: POSSIBLE SOLUTION

U.S. Presence in Global Affairs

Complete the chart by writing several sentences to describe each organization. Explain how and why the United States is involved in international affairs.

U.S. Involvement in International Affairs

	Who?	What?	How it solves problems?	Why?
United Nations (UN)	*delegates from 50 nations*	*an organization intended to preserve world peace*	*addresses military and political problems around the globe that could lead to conflict*	*an understanding of possibility of new global conflicts; after WWII, a clear understanding of the crucial need to avoid these conflicts*
North Atlantic Treaty Organization (NATO)	*nine Western European nations, Canada, Iceland, and the United States*	*a military organization pledged to defend the participating countries*	*by sending military forces into trouble spots*	*Conflicts with Soviets in Berlin convinced Western powers that military force might be needed to suppress further conflicts.*
Central Intelligence Agency (CIA)	*U.S. government agency*	*an organization to implement covert actions abroad*	*gathers military and political information; foments and aids coups; promotes leadership favorable to U.S.; shapes world events through internal intervention*	*The Cold War and assumed threat of the spread of communism convinced U.S leaders they needed to be informed of global events.*
National Security Council (NSC)	*advisers to the president*	*presidential advisory committee on military and political affairs*	*informed advice to the president*	*Events after WWII and the Cold War required president to stay abreast of complicated world events and military/political tactics.*

Name ______________________ Class ____________ Date ____________

CHAPTER 29

Society After World War II

GRAPHIC ORGANIZER ACTIVITY

Voices of Dissent

Complete the graphic organizer by listing the dissatisfactions with American society expressed by each group in the 1950s.

Dissatisfactions with American Society

African Americans	Hispanics

Asian Americans	American Indians

Society After World War II

GRAPHIC ORGANIZER: POSSIBLE SOLUTION

Voices of Dissent

Complete the graphic organizer by listing the dissatisfactions with American society expressed by each group in the 1950s.

Dissatisfactions with American Society

African Americans	Hispanics
Segregated schools forced African Americans to travel long distances and attend substandard schools, lowering self-worth and quality of education. *White communities protested integration and threatened students.* *African Americans were forced to ride in the back of buses.*	*Texas town refused to bury body of Mexican American soldier.* *California and Texas schools were segregated.* *In cities, Hispanics found prejudice, poverty, and poor housing.*
Asian Americans	**American Indians**
racism in suburbs of San Francisco	*American Indians were relocated to cities as reservations were terminated. Tribal leaders feared loss of culture and future leaders.*

Name ______________________ Class ____________ Date ____________

The New Frontier and the Great Society

GRAPHIC ORGANIZER ACTIVITY

The Cuban Missile Crisis

Complete the graphic organizer with information about the Cuban missile crisis.

The Cuban Missile Crisis

EXPLAIN the relationship between the United States and the Soviet Union in 1959.

WHAT was Kennedy's first move against communist Cuba?

WHY did he think this plan would succeed?

WHAT did Khrushchev do in support of Fidel Castro?

WHY did Khrushchev think he could accomplish this task?

WHAT was the outcome of the Cuban missile crisis?

The New Frontier and the Great Society

GRAPHIC ORGANIZER: POSSIBLE SOLUTION

The Cuban Missile Crisis

Complete the graphic organizer with information about the Cuban missile crisis.

The Cuban Missile Crisis

EXPLAIN the relationship between the United States and the Soviet Union in 1959.

The United States was concerned that communism would spread throughout the world, including in the Western Hemisphere.

WHAT was Kennedy's first move against communist Cuba?

He invaded Cuba with CIA-trained anti-Castro Cuban refugees.

WHY did he think this plan would succeed?

Kennedy was following Eisenhower's plan.

WHAT did Khrushchev do in support of Fidel Castro?

He agreed to provide Cuba with nuclear missiles; shipped the missiles to Cuba.

WHY did Khrushchev think he could accomplish this task?

Kennedy had appeared weak at the Bay of Pigs and in the Berlin Wall incident.

WHAT was the outcome of the Cuban missile crisis?

Both sides compromised; Soviet ships turned around. In 1963 the United States, Britain, and the Soviet Union signed the Limited Nuclear Test Ban Treaty, limiting nuclear testing. The superpowers also established better communication in the form of a "hot line."

Name ______________________ Class ____________ Date ____________

The Civil Rights Movement

GRAPHIC ORGANIZER ACTIVITY

In the Words of the Leaders

Complete the graphic organizer by identifying the civil rights leader quoted in each section and explaining the position expressed.

Quotation	
"I have earnestly opposed violent tension, but there is a type of constructive, nonviolent tension which is necessary for growth. . . ."	
"If you drive a panther into a corner, if he can't go left and he can't go right, then he will tend to come out of that corner to wipe out or stop its aggressor." "Black people will not be free until we are free to determine our own destiny."	
"It was then that I began to change—inside." "by any means necessary. . . ."	
"What do you want? Black Power!"	

The Civil Rights Movement

GRAPHIC ORGANIZER: POSSIBLE SOLUTION

In the Words of the Leaders

Complete the graphic organizer by identifying the civil rights leader quoted in each section and explaining the position expressed.

Quotation	Leader and Position
"I have earnestly opposed violent tension, but there is a type of constructive, nonviolent tension which is necessary for growth. . . ."	*Martin Luther King Jr., who believed continued nonviolent demonstrations would create the tension necessary to eradicate racism. He believed a nonviolent approach was necessary to maintain human dignity.*
"If you drive a panther into a corner, if he can't go left and he can't go right, then he will tend to come out of that corner to wipe out or stop its aggressor." "Black people will not be free until we are free to determine our own destiny."	*Bobby Seale, on why he chose the name Black Panthers.* *Seale believed in confrontation as the only way to eradicate racism. He created black self-defense groups to protect communities from police oppression.*
"It was then that I began to change—inside." "by any means necessary . . ."	*Malcolm X. The first quotation was a response to a teacher who stated that a law career was an unrealistic goal for an African American.* *Malcolm X advocated fighting for one's beliefs. He had strong and radical views on violent protest. He later followed a more traditional Islamic belief in acceptance.*
"What do you want? Black Power!"	*Stokely Carmichael advocated African American cultural separatism. He promoted racial pride and pride in African culture.*

Name ________________ Class ________ Date ________

Struggles for Change

GRAPHIC ORGANIZER ACTIVITY

Protesting the Status Quo

Create protest signs explaining why members of each group were dissatisfied with American society in the 1960s.

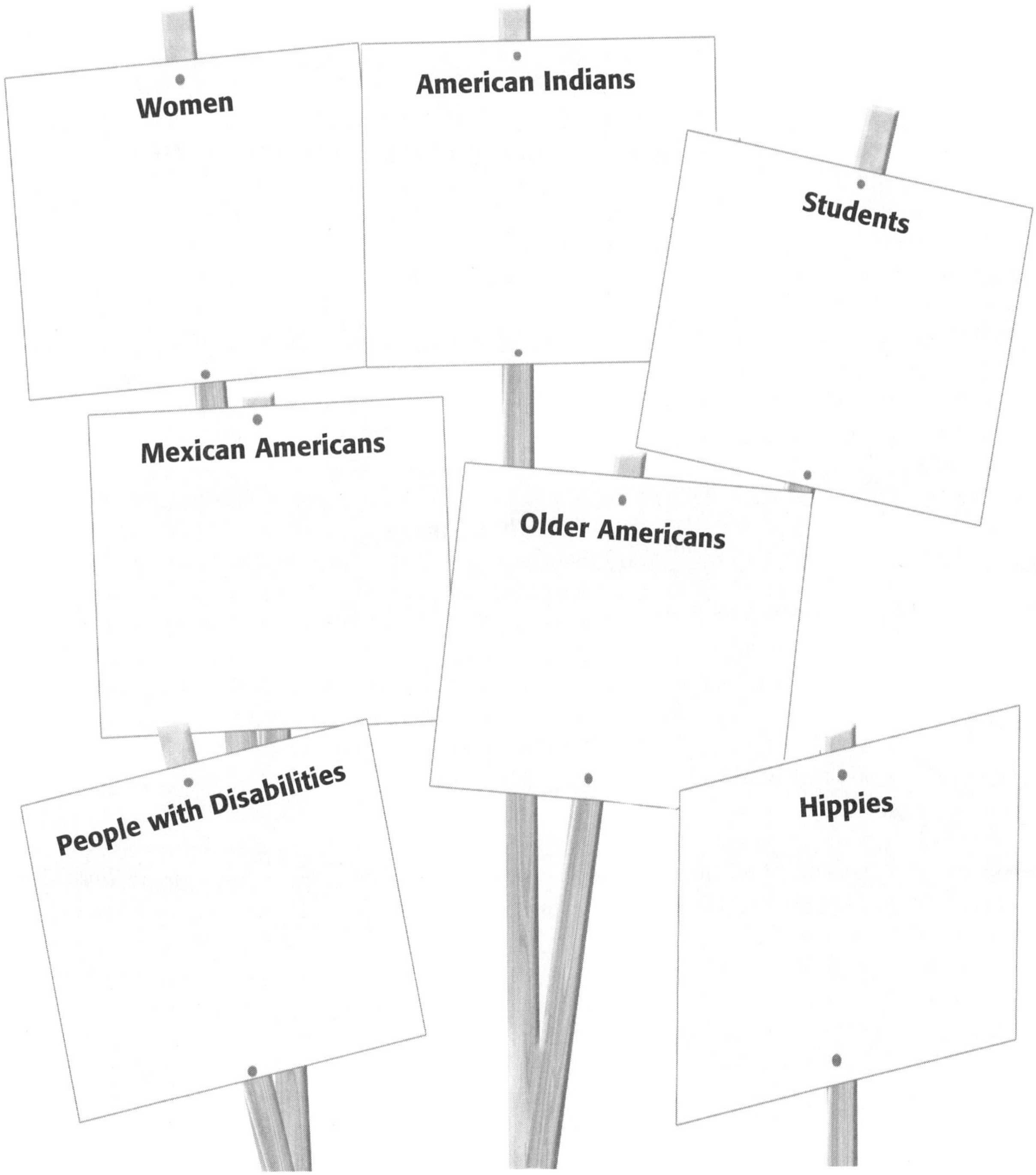

Women

American Indians

Students

Mexican Americans

Older Americans

People with Disabilities

Hippies

Struggles for Change

GRAPHIC ORGANIZER: POSSIBLE SOLUTION

Protesting the Status Quo

Create protest signs explaining why members of each group were dissatisfied with American society in the 1960s.

Women

complained of unfulfilled lives; unfair treatment in the workplace; low wages; sexual discrimination in education, employment, and sports; cultural assumption of male superiority

American Indians

extreme poverty on the reservations; loss of tribal rights and culture; wanted hearings on broken treaties and BIA misconduct; wanted to recover sacred lands

Students

demanded right to free speech at UC Berkeley and other universities; protested for civil rights and against the war in Vietnam

Mexican Americans

extremely low wages; backbreaking labor; migrant lifestyle; provided no facilities for education, health; wanted to regain land rights in New Mexico; faced racism, police brutality

Older Americans

opposed mandatory retirement, age discrimination; wanted better health care

People with Disabilities

could not use facilities their tax dollars had paid for; children with disabilities could not attend regular schools

Hippies

rejected materialism; dropped out of society; lived communally; experimented with drugs and sexual permissiveness; rejected conservative clothing, music, lifestyle

CHAPTER 33

Name ______________________ Class __________ Date __________

War in Vietnam

GRAPHIC ORGANIZER ACTIVITY

A Divided Nation

Complete the chart by describing the opposing viewpoints held by Americans during the Vietnam War. Then write a paragraph describing which viewpoint you might have agreed with at the time. Explain your choice.

Hawks' Viewpoints	Doves' Viewpoints
•	•
•	•
•	•
•	•
•	•
•	•

In the late 1960s my opinion would have been

____

____

____

____

____

War in Vietnam

GRAPHIC ORGANIZER: POSSIBLE SOLUTION

A Divided Nation

Complete the chart by describing the opposing viewpoints held by Americans during the Vietnam War. Then write a paragraph describing which viewpoint you might have agreed with at the time. Explain your choice.

Hawks' Viewpoints	Doves' Viewpoints
• *supported the war's goals: to stop the spread of communism* • *believed any U.S. defeat humiliating* • *believed the United States could win the war* • *wanted more U.S. troops and heavier bombing* • *believed that the U.S. government would act in our best interests*	• *After the Tet Offensive, people understood that the war could drag on indefinitely.* • *strong support for nonviolence, belief that all war was wrong* • *did not want to risk their lives for a distant cause* • *Increased protests and police violence began destroying America.* • *The Pentagon Papers revealed that the government had concealed facts about the war.* • *felt that the war aims were against the wishes of a majority of Vietnamese*

In the late 1960s my opinion would have been

Answers may vary. Students should use the viewpoints mentioned in the chart to support their opinion.

Name ________________ Class ________ Date ________

CHAPTER 34

From Nixon to Carter

GRAPHIC ORGANIZER ACTIVITY

The Nixon Administration

Complete the graphic organizer by describing the different aspects of the Nixon presidency.

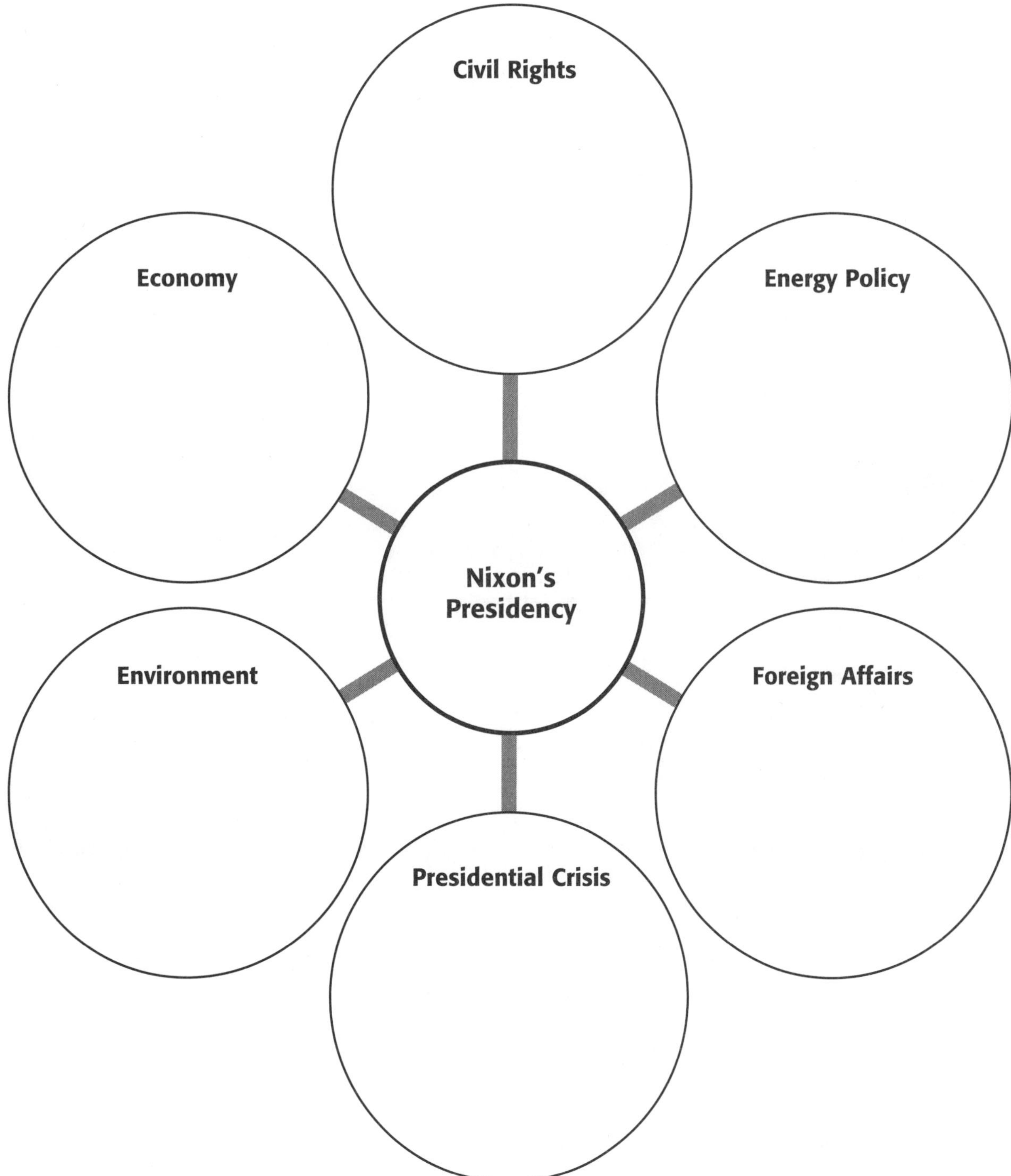

From Nixon to Carter

GRAPHIC ORGANIZER: POSSIBLE SOLUTION

The Nixon Administration

Complete the graphic organizer by describing the different aspects of the Nixon presidency.

Nixon's Presidency

Civil Rights
- *appointed conservative justices*
- *steered away from civil rights, opposed busing*

Economy
- *because of concern about stagflation, imposed wage and price controls*

Energy Policy
- *To decrease dependence on foreign energy sources, Nixon reduced highway speeds, authorized the Alaskan pipeline, and increased support for nuclear energy sources.*

Environment
- *established Environmental Protection Agency*
- *passed the Clean Air Act, Water Quality Improvement Act, and Endangered Species Act*

Foreign Affairs
- *realpolitik: national interests over moral or ethical concerns*
- *eased tensions with China and the Soviet Union*
- *sent CIA to disrupt Chilean socialist government*

Presidential Crisis
- *shifted authority to cabinet*
- *hid information from Congress*
- *authorized the burglary of Democratic headquarters*
- *destroyed evidence*

Name ______________________ Class __________ Date __________

The Republican Revolution

GRAPHIC ORGANIZER ACTIVITY

Economics in the 1980s

Complete the graphic organizer by describing each term in the spaces provided.

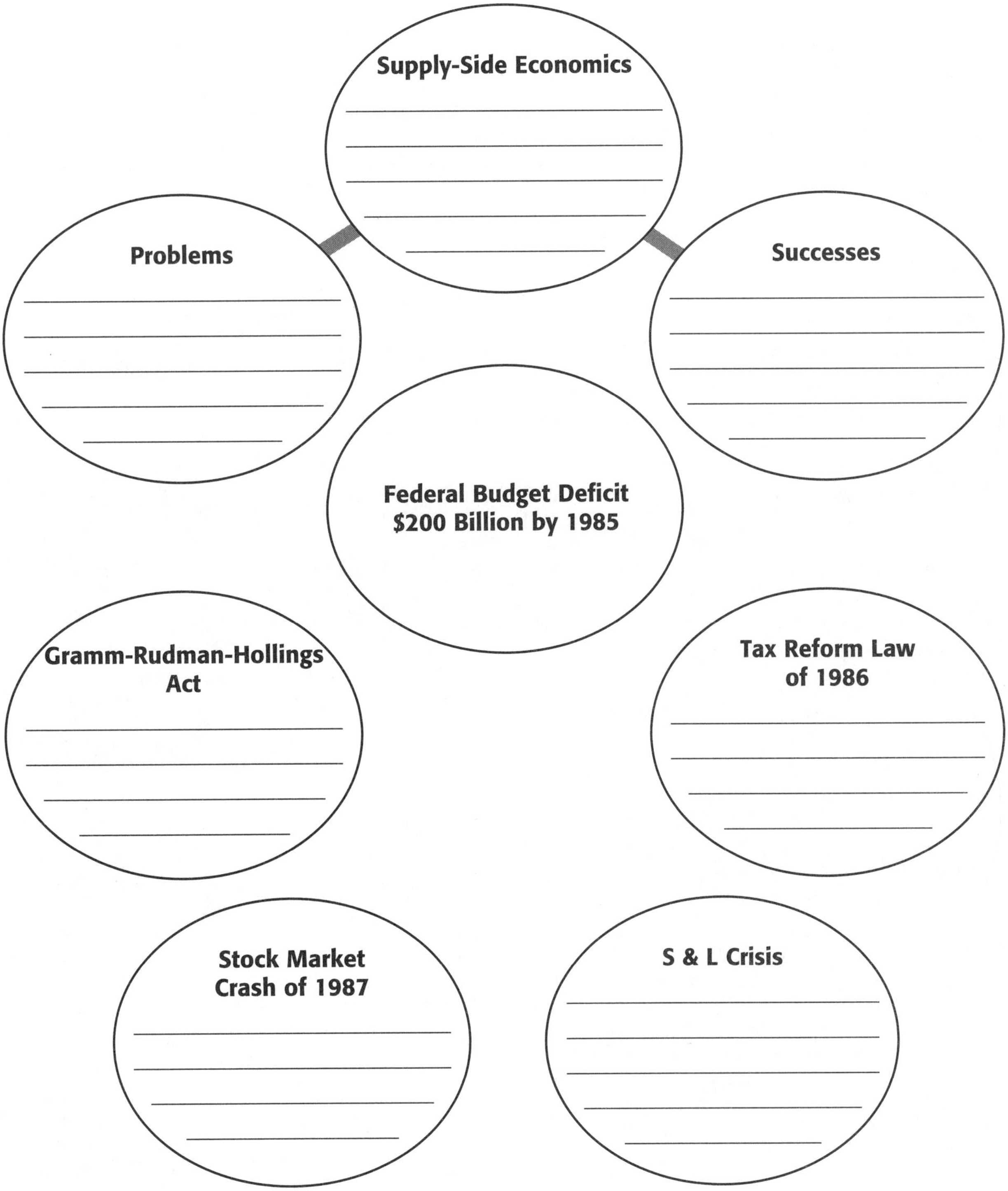

Supply-Side Economics

____
____
____
____
____

Problems

____
____
____
____
____

Successes

____
____
____
____
____

**Federal Budget Deficit
$200 Billion by 1985**

Gramm-Rudman-Hollings Act

____
____
____
____

Tax Reform Law of 1986

____
____
____
____

Stock Market Crash of 1987

____
____
____
____

S & L Crisis

____
____
____
____
____

The Republican Revolution

GRAPHIC ORGANIZER: POSSIBLE SOLUTION

Economics in the 1980s

Complete the graphic organizer by describing each term in the spaces provided.

Supply-Side Economics

cut federal taxes to induce investment in business and hiring to stimulate economy

increased spending on the military to lessen communist threat

Problems

the poorest Americans became poorer; homelessness increased; lower taxes and increased government spending increased budget deficit

Successes

stimulated business and employment; decrease in inflation;

stock market boom

Federal Budget Deficit $200 Billion by 1985

Gramm-Rudman-Hollings Act

required automatic cuts in government spending

Tax Reform Law of 1986

eliminated special tax breaks groups had received

Stock Market Crash of 1987

insider trading; use of confidential information to make huge profits

S & L Crisis

Freed of federal regulations, savings and loan banks issued risky loans; banks failed.

CHAPTER 36

Name ______________________ Class ____________ Date ____________

Launching the New Millennium

GRAPHIC ORGANIZER ACTIVITY

The Serbian Conflict

Study the map. Then describe events that occurred in each region during the date marked.

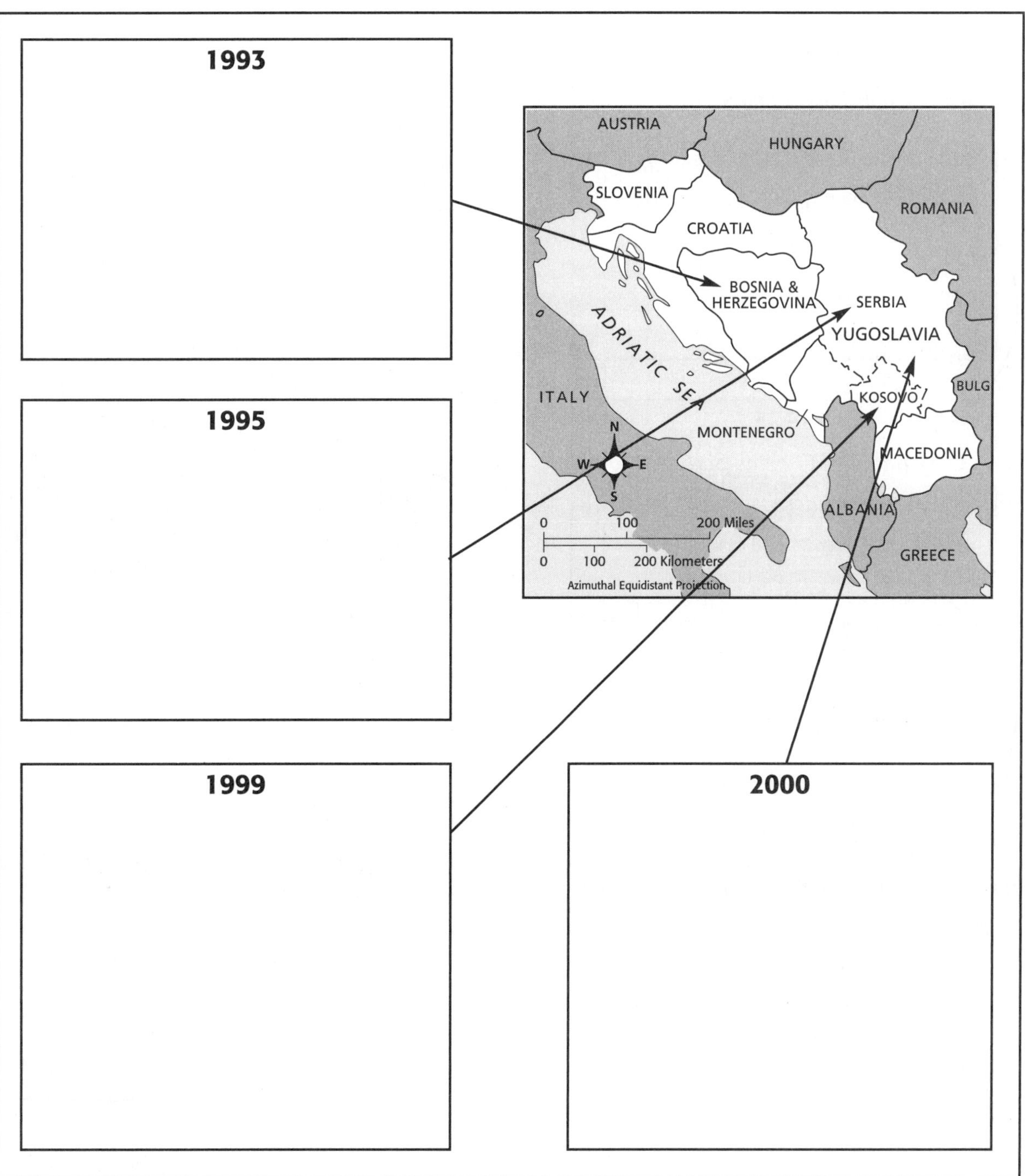

Launching the New Millennium

GRAPHIC ORGANIZER: POSSIBLE SOLUTION

The Serbian Conflict

Study the map. Then describe events that occurred in each region during the date marked.

1993

- *Ethnic fighting among Serbs, Croatians, and Slovenes occurs in Bosnia and Herzegovina. UN and NATO send in peacekeeping forces.*

1995

- *U.S. and NATO bomb Serb positions.*
- *U.S. brings leaders together for a peace accord.*

1999

- *Serbs resume violence, murdering Albanians and forcing them from their homes. NATO begins air strikes against Yugoslavia.*
- *Milosevic withdraws forces.*
- *NATO troops are stationed in the region to preserve peace and allow Albanians to return home.*

2000

- *Voters elect Vojislav Kostunica as their new president. Milosevic refuses to accept defeat.*
- *Hundreds of thousands of Serbians demonstrate against Milosevic. Milosevic accepts defeat.*

AUSTRIA
HUNGARY
SLOVENIA
CROATIA
ROMANIA
BOSNIA & HERZEGOVINA
SERBIA
YUGOSLAVIA
ADRIATIC SEA
ITALY
KOSOVO
BULG
MONTENEGRO
MACEDONIA
ALBANIA
GREECE
N
W
E
S
0 100 200 Miles
0 100 200 Kilometers
Azimuthal Equidistant Projection